D0857992

# Sequoyah's Gift

A PORTRAIT OF THE CHEROKEE LEADER

# Sequoyah's Gift

## A PORTRAIT OF THE CHEROKEE LEADER

*By Janet Klausner*

WITH AN AFTERWORD BY DUANE H. KING

HarperCollins*Publishers*

The photographs used in this book are from the following sources and are used with their permission:

American Antiquarian Society, p. 63; Bob Annesley, for his sculpture *Sequoyah and Ahyokah* and his painting *Sequoyah's Dream*, photos by Ken Krueger: pp. 51, 87; Architect of the Capitol, U.S. Capitol Art Collection, p. 92; Thomas Gilcrease Institute of American History and Art, Tulsa, Oklahoma: pp. 59, 79; B. Haskins/J. Hamley: pp. 58, 65, 67; National Portrait Gallery, Smithsonian Institution, p. 37; Oklahoma Historical Society, Archives and Manuscripts Division, pp. 35, 60, 71, 75, 91; Smithsonian Institution, photo number 44, 654, p. 28; United States Postal Service, for the stamp "Sequoyah" © 1980, p. 94; University of Oklahoma Press, for a page from *Beginning Cherokee*, by Ruth Bradley Holmes and Betty Sharp Smith. Copyright © 1976, 1977 by the University of Oklahoma Press. p. 56; Woodenturtle (Christopher Nyerges), p. 96; Woolaroc Museum, Bartlesville, Oklahoma, p. x.

 Printed in the United States of America. For information address HarperCollins Children's Books, a division of HarperCollins Publishers, 10 East 53rd Street, New York, NY 10022.
Typography by Al Cetta
1 2 3 4 5 6 7 8 9 10
❖
First Edition

Library of Congress Cataloging-in-Publication Data
Klausner, Janet.
Sequoyah's gift : a portrait of the Cherokee leader / by Janet Klausner ; with an afterword by Duane H. King.
p. cm.
Includes bibliographical references (p. ).
Summary: A biography of the Cherokee Indian who created a method for his people to write and read their own language.
ISBN 0-06-021235-7. — ISBN 0-06-021236-5 (lib. bdg.)
1. Sequoyah, 1770?–1843—Juvenile literature. 2. Cherokee Indians—Biography—Juvenile literature. 3. Cherokee Indians—Writing—Juvenile literature. 4. Cherokee language—Writing—Juvenile literature. [1. Sequoyah, 1770?–1843. 2. Cherokee Indians—Biography. 3. Indians of North America—Biography.] I. Title.
E99.C5S3846 1993 92-24939
973'.0497502—dc20 CIP
[B] AC

*For Jeff Hamley*

With thanks for their advice and encouragement to
Joanne Fedorocko, Wendy Gaal, Bette Haskins,
Duane H. King, and Katherine Tegen.

# Contents

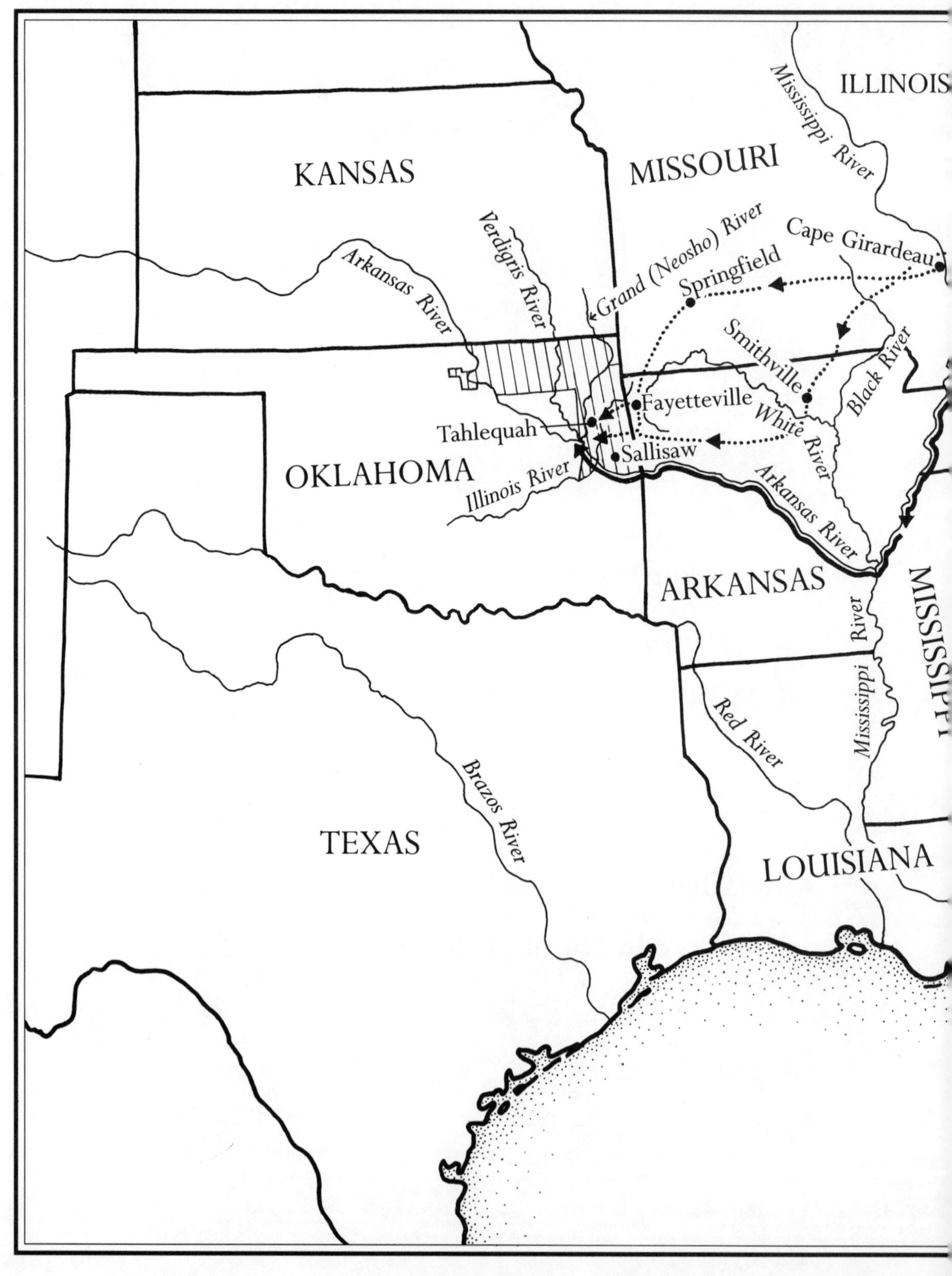
ILLINOIS
Mississippi River
KANSAS
MISSOURI
Verdigris River
Grand (Neosho) River
Cape Girardeau
Arkansas River
Springfield
Smithville
Black River
Fayetteville
White River
Tahlequah
Sallisaw
OKLAHOMA
Illinois River
Arkansas River
ARKANSAS
MISSISSIPPI
River
Mississippi
Red River
Brazos River
TEXAS
LOUISIANA

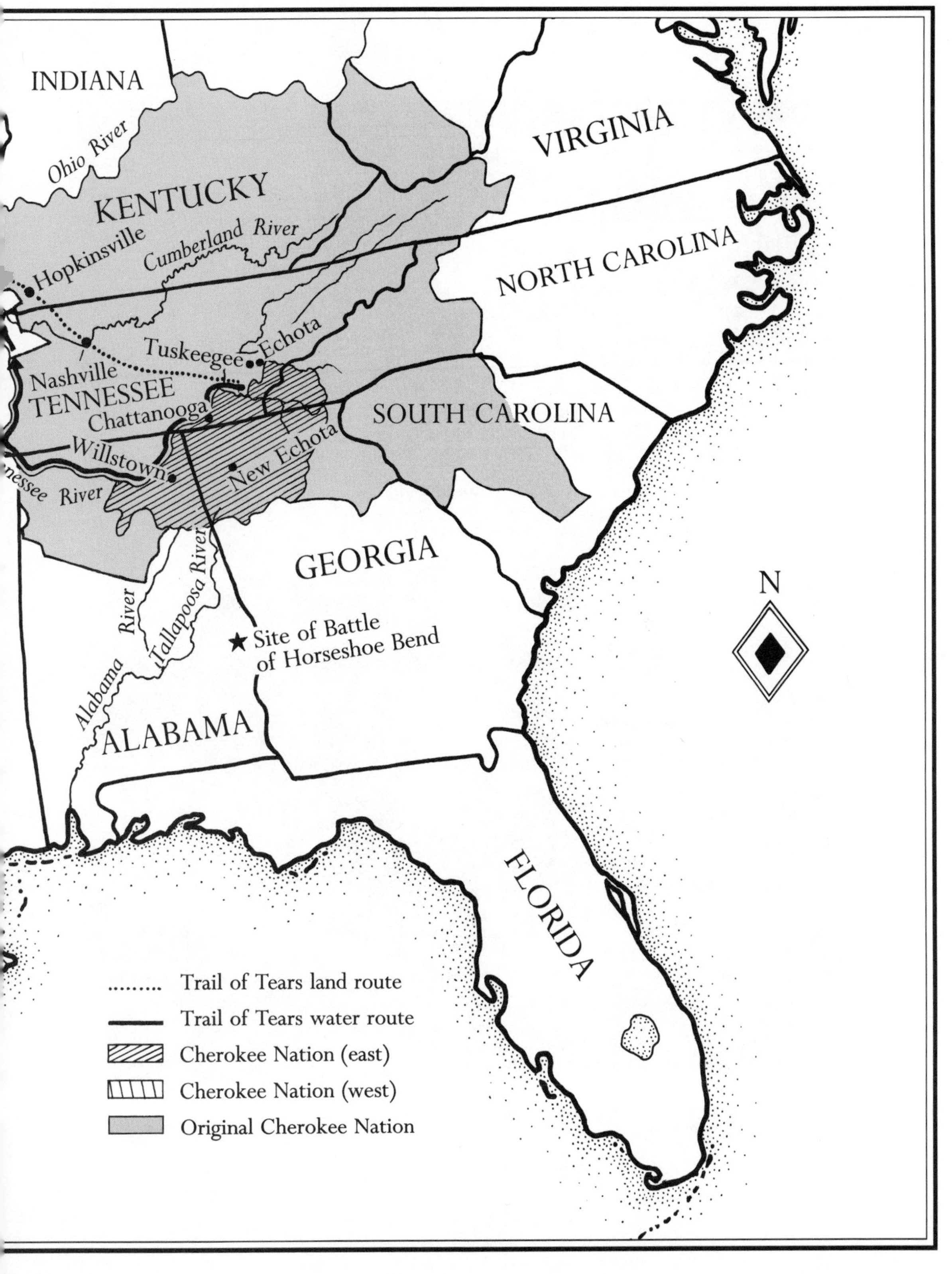
INDIANA
Ohio River
KENTUCKY
Hopkinsville
Cumberland River
VIRGINIA
NORTH CAROLINA
Nashville
Tuskeegee
Echota
TENNESSEE
Chattanooga
SOUTH CAROLINA
Willstown
New Echota
River
GEORGIA
Tallapoosa River
River
Alabama
Site of Battle
of Horseshoe Bend
ALABAMA
N
FLORIDA
Trail of Tears land route
Trail of Tears water route
Cherokee Nation (east)
Cherokee Nation (west)
Original Cherokee Nation

Sequoyah as depicted by the painter Robert Lindneux in 1940.

# Author's Note

This book is an account of the life, times, and achievements of a man called Sequoyah, who lived two hundred years ago. Sequoyah was a real person, but he was also a legend—even in his own lifetime. As with all legends, it is difficult to separate fact from fiction.

Most information about who Sequoyah was and what he did comes from reports made by people who knew him or met him. I have relied on those reports in the writing of this book. The conversations shown in quotation marks are those noted in historical documents. Conversations and thoughts that *might* have occurred are shown without quotation marks.

We can only guess at Sequoyah's own thoughts. Although he was often seen writing in his journal, very few of his writing samples have surfaced. It has been said that his journals were buried with him. Documents that give evidence about his year of birth, his childhood, his marriages and children, and much else are limited. But we can still know him—by discovering what his world was like and by thinking about the remarkable things he did.

# Sequoyah's Gift
## A PORTRAIT OF THE CHEROKEE LEADER

# One
# A Way of Life

On a day more than two hundred years ago, when the Cherokees were still masters of a large region of the American Southeast, a Cherokee messenger rode through the countryside. He stopped at the farmstead belonging to a woman called Wuh-teh. A small boy was by Wuh-teh's side, listening with an alert face as the rider spoke the news. Something important was happening several miles away in Echota, the sacred town that was the capital of the Cherokees. When the messenger finished explaining, Wuh-teh turned to her son. We will go to Echota, she told him.

When they arrived, they gathered with all the other Cherokees who had heard the message. A delegation from the Iroquois, far to the north, was coming to the town. A peace delegation. Finally there would be peace between the two peoples, after a century of raids and killings. Wuh-teh wanted to witness the event. She wanted her small son to see it with her. Perhaps he would remember the moment.

While the people in Echota waited for the Iroquois delegates to arrive, they talked about what had happened when the delegates crossed the Tennessee River into Cherokee territory. The Iroquois men lost their way, and instead of arriving first at Echota, where no violence was allowed, they arrived at a different town to the south. They came to the cabin of the town chief. He was not at home. But his daughter did what was customary when strangers came by—she set out food for them. When her father came back, he was astonished to see these enemies in his house. Just as they were explaining they were peace delegates, several Cherokee men, armed and ready for battle, were at the door. The chief managed to stop them from attacking the guests. After the delegates rested, he led them fifteen miles north to Echota.

The boy and his mother listened with interest to the story of the narrow escape. Then they watched as the Iroquois men walked calmly through the town square. The men came to the town house, a huge, circular building with a dome roof. Inside the town house, the Iroquois delegates spoke to the Cherokee people. They told of the peace agreement that had been made several years earlier. They said they had waited until the time was right to make the agreement final, and now that time had come. They had brought with them several belts strung with wampum, cylindrical beads made from shells. The shells were arranged in colored patterns, and the patterns were symbolic—they stood for meanings.

The boy watched the delegates hold up the wampum belts and explain their importance. He watched as the belts and other tokens of friendship were passed into Cherokee hands. He stayed with his mother for the feasting and dancing that followed. He was too young to understand fully, but he knew that something wonderful had taken place. As the years passed, he would listen to recountings of the event. And he would know why the wampum belts were so valuable. They contained the talk of peace. The Cherokees would treasure them and pass them down to succeeding generations. For the rest of his life, the boy would remember what he had witnessed.

The Iroquois peace delegation arrived in Cherokee country in the early 1770's. The Cherokee boy who would later recall their arrival was Sequoyah.

Sequoyah spent his early years with his mother in what is now eastern Tennessee. Sequoyah's father was a white man—a trader or a soldier—who had left the Cherokee community before Sequoyah knew him. As was the custom for Cherokee boys, Sequoyah looked to his mother's brothers for guidance and instruction. His uncles were leaders among the Cherokees. One uncle held the honored position of town chief in the sacred capital.

Sequoyah grew up in mountain country. When the Cherokee elders described how the world began, they told about the Great Buzzard, who had flapped his wings against the soft mud of the just-formed earth. With each wingstroke down, the Great Buzzard created a valley, and with each stroke up he created a mountain. It was because of the Great Buzzard that Cherokee country was so full of mountains.

The Cherokee homelands are rugged but also lush and generous. The peaks are draped under a bluish mist. Today the Cherokee hills are known as the Great Smoky Mountains, or the Great Smokies.

As a boy, Sequoyah climbed the mountain trails, his soft deerskin moccasins silently gripping the earth. He walked among the towering yellow poplars and the strong white oaks, the sweet gum trees and the willows draping their leaves over rushing streams.

He learned how the world changes with the changing seasons. In the fall and winter, when crunching frost or snow covered the ground, he gathered nuts—hickory, chestnuts, walnuts, and acorns that could be ground into meal. In the spring he waited for the winter ice to break and the streams to fill with roaring water. He listened curiously to the loud waterfalls and wondered about the conversations that the Thunder people might be having under them. Sequoyah listened for the thunderclaps and the pelting rain that came every year to wash the whole world clean. Colorful flowers then spilled from the mountainsides—irises, rhododendrons, wild tiger lilies. In summer he gathered blackberries and huckleberries and strawberries.

He learned to recognize birds by their songs and to spot their nests in the trees. He learned how and where the turtles and the otters and the deer lived. Like all Cherokee children, he spent hours playing in the woods, learning by watching, listening, thinking. At an early age, Sequoyah was setting traps for turkeys and baiting baskets for fish. The forests were filled with deer, rabbits, raccoons, and bears. Herds of mountain buffalo still wandered in the region when Sequoyah was young. He herded wild colts from the woods to his mother's farmstead and cared for them until they were ready to be broken.

He learned how to shape a blowgun out of a hollow reed and to whittle twigs into darts. He practiced at targets and joined his cousins and friends as they used their blowguns to hunt squirrels. When Sequoyah became older, he used a muzzle-loading gun for larger game, perhaps a flintlock musket or a rifle that Wuh-teh had traded for furs she collected from hunters.

Boys learned early to trap, hunt, and fish. Meat was an important part of the Cherokee diet. But the Cherokees were also farmers, and their most valuable staple was corn.

Sequoyah's mother took him into their cornfield in spring and showed him how to touch and smell the soil to tell whether it was warm enough for planting. She taught him how to use a hoe. He helped fill the earth with their seed corn.

There were other vegetables to plant and raise—beans, cabbage, pumpkin, squash. Sequoyah also helped his mother tend and milk her cows. He looked after the hogs in the hogpen and the chickens in the henhouse.

Sequoyah always found something to occupy himself with,

even if it was just sitting quietly by a stream studying the patterns made by water beetles and listening to the wind in the trees. Since neighbors lived far away, he often spent time alone. He liked to work with his hands and entertained himself by building toy houses of twigs. Sometimes he sat with a sheet of bark against his knees and made sketches with a piece of charcoal, the edge of a rock, or a knife point. He liked watching the image of an animal take shape. His hands usually did what he told them, but sometimes the creature did not come out the way he wished, and he would try again. When he showed his completed deer or buffalo or horse to his mother, she smiled with pleasure, and he knew that he had done well.

She was also proud of him because he seemed always to be planning, thinking, figuring things out. Once he surprised her by constructing a small wooden building over a spring, to serve as a cold storehouse for the milk and cream from her dairy cows.

He was still a child when people began to speak of his talents. The boy has unusual abilities, they said. They talked about how helpful Sequoyah was and how well he was growing up.

The Cherokee farmsteads were spread out through the hollows and flatlands. Many dwellings were miles from the town center. Sequoyah's town, some distance from his home, was Tah-skee-gee, on the Little Tennessee River. In the town, as in all Cherokee towns, there was a grain storehouse as well as community gardens of corn and beans to be shared with the needy or with visitors. The most important building in the town was the circular town house, large enough to hold five hundred people. Councils were held there. Next to it was a square for ceremonies and celebrations. Sequoyah looked forward to the gatherings and festivals held in Tah-skee-gee. Even though there were few people near his home, Sequoyah and his mother still felt part of the community. Social and religious gatherings made it possible for distant neighbors to remain close.

Sequoyah's sense of anticipation began to build in midsummer, when the young corn—the green corn—had soft and pulpy kernels and was ready for roasting. Soon the call would come to assemble in the town for the first of the Green Corn ceremonies. He knew, as all Cherokee children knew, that it was terribly wrong to pluck any corn yet. Until the festivals were over, the corn belonged to the spirit powers. The people could not yet claim ownership of the corn, even though they had planted it. As the roasting-ear time neared, Sequoyah waited expectantly. At last a day came when he heard sharp shouts in the distance, the signal that someone was approaching. A runner appeared, and Sequoyah went to him eagerly.

Yes, this was the messenger sent by the Council leaders. The time has come, he told Sequoyah and Wuh-teh. It is time to gather together in the town.

Sequoyah, his mother, his uncles and aunts, his cousins, and everyone else now had to prepare themselves. People gathered in groups on the bank of a stream. Then each person stepped into the flowing water. Sequoyah dipped his body in once, twice, then again and again, until he reached the count of seven. After he came out of the water, he stood still as his uncle used a sharp bone to make scratches on his chest, back, arms, and legs. His uncle put the ritual scratches on other family members too. Then Sequoyah took his turn drinking a special liquid made from plant roots. By going to water, by accepting the scratches that bled, by swallowing the medicine, Sequoyah made himself pure of spirit.

When the religious leaders sacrificed the seven ears of corn in the sacred oak fire burning in the center of the town house, all those who were purified could participate in the festival. There was no time of year with greater importance.

Sequoyah listened to the songs of thankfulness in the town square. He swayed back and forth following the motions of the men and women dancing solemnly in their separate lines. He stayed up all night laughing with his cousins and eating corn and fresh meat until his stomach bulged and he could not swallow another bite. Then he and his mother returned home, tired and satisfied. Now they could eat the young corn from their fields.

Corn continued growing until autumn, when it became fully ripe and hard. Then another ceremony was held. This one lasted several days, with many different kinds of dances. A new sacred fire was kindled in the town house, and Sequoyah's mother took part of that fire home with her.

The ceremonies brought a sense of renewal and hope. Everyone made a personal promise to try harder in the coming year—to be honorable, to live in harmony with others, to be fair and generous, to be a better human being. These were the values that were shared by the *ah-nee-YUH-wee-yah*, "the real people," as the Cherokees called themselves. These were the values that Sequoyah learned while he was growing up.

When the Green Corn ceremonies were going on, Council meetings were also held in the town. From the time he was old enough to understand, Sequoyah listened with awe to the speakers at Council. The people held deep respect for anyone with the ability to speak wisely and persuasively. A great leader was often a fearless warrior, who had had success in battle. But it was not necessary to achieve glory in war if one could wield the spoken word with force. A speaker stood tall, fingers interlocked, hands and arms unmoving. Using words and voice alone—no gestures—he would recite or recount or explain or persuade. He would send his words deep inside his audience. A skilled speaker could improvise an argument on the spot, making points smoothly, poetically, and with a sincerity that touched all listeners. And when he was done, they would say *doh-HYU-hnoh*, "It is true."

The Cherokees, like all native peoples north of Mexico, relied on the spoken word to pass down their traditions and their system of beliefs. The storytellers and the healers recited from memory.

All knowledge—from histories that took hours to recite to formulas for healing illness—all was memorized and repeated.

Some of the myths that were passed from generation to generation were sacred, valuable, and shared only by a chosen few. When nights were cold, the healers would often gather in the *oh-see*, a small hothouse, to share their secret knowledge. But other tales could be told anytime and anywhere.

As a boy, Sequoyah settled down with delight whenever an elder began with the familiar opening: "This is what the old men told me when I was a boy." No one tired of hearing the animal tales. There were many stories about Rabbit, the trickster who was often too smart for his own good.

In one tale, Rabbit was caught trying to cheat in a race against Deer. He was discovered clearing a path through the thicket that was to be the racecourse. The animals decided to give the prize, a pair of antlers, to the Deer, who has worn them ever since.

Along with the other listeners, Sequoyah smiled with satisfaction as the storyteller came to the ending: "They told the Rabbit that, as he was so fond of cutting down bushes, he might thereafter do that for a living—and so he does to this day."

The tales were good entertainment, of course, but they also taught lessons—about the importance of honesty, about the weak overcoming the strong.

Stories and ceremonies held the Cherokee people together. The sense of community was strengthened with other social gatherings during the year. When the town chief announced a common dance, everyone joined in. At the head of the line was the singer, stamping and setting the pace. Behind him stamped others, including women wearing ankle rattles made of pebbles inside terrapin shells. And stepping rhythmically at the end of the line were the children, Sequoyah among them.

There were also sports events. The most famous Cherokee sport was *ah-NEH-jah*, the ball play. The ball play was not simply a game. It was a serious matter, requiring many rituals. The athletes were specially selected for skill and strength. Their training was demanding. Secret preparations began weeks in advance of a game. The teams usually represented different towns, and a town's prestige and honor were at stake.

The ball play was most like the modern game of lacrosse, which originated with Native Americans. In the Cherokee ball play, each player held two sticks made of bent hickory. Each stick was shaped like a three-foot-long spoon, with the bowl part made of leather thongs. The ball was covered with deerskin. The object of the game was to drive the ball between the goalposts to score a run, and to win by making twelve runs.

Sequoyah attended the ball plays, along with all the other devoted and boisterous fans. He shouted enthusiastically as pairs of players from opposing teams jabbed, wrestled, tripped, threw, and hammered each other as hard as they could. The game began with the players' prayer, "Grant me such strength in the contest that my enemy may be of no weight in my hands—that I may be able to toss him into the air or dash him to the earth." It quickly became a ferocious battle.

A game could go on for hours. The spectators, excited with town pride, bet heavily. Horses, clothing, jewelry—all sorts of goods could be lost or gained at a ball game. It was no wonder that successful players became town heroes.

Even as he thrilled to the players' strength and speed, Sequoyah knew he would never participate in the game. He would never be one of the strong young men selected to represent the town. Sequoyah had the full use of only one leg. A childhood accident or illness had caused the muscles of one leg to weaken, and Sequoyah walked with a limp.

Sequoyah did not let this weakness limit his activity. He rode a horse skillfully. He walked and climbed and hunted. He plowed fields and chopped firewood and performed all the other labors required on a farm. There were many useful paths open to him. Life was full of good things as Sequoyah was growing up. But there were troubling matters too.

# Two
# A Reputation

Even as the Cherokees were making peace with the Iroquois, they were at war with other enemies. The Cherokees had always been proud and accomplished fighters. The people admired bravery and success in battle. It was the goal of every young man to show himself fearless in the face of danger. Warriors often proved themselves in raids and combat against the Creeks and other native peoples of the region. But new enemies were posing an enormous threat to Cherokee homelands. These enemies were white intruders from the American colonies.

As white settlers attempted to set up homes in Cherokee territory, warriors attacked. They burned the settlers' cabins and killed whole families. The settlers fought back. They sought revenge and protection. Armies of Americans from the Carolinas, Virginia, and Georgia were brought in to subdue the Cherokees.

Sequoyah was a young boy when word came of the approach of the white soldiers. These were dangerous men who shot children and women and took their scalps. They made prisoners of the Cherokees and then killed them or sold them into slavery. Sequoyah and his mother and all their neighbors abandoned their farms and headed into the mountains. Their own warriors were fighting elsewhere, and there were too few here to protect them. Sequoyah waited silently and listened. From their campsites and cave shelters, the people heard violent shouts and gunfire echoing below. They heard bellowing cattle being stampeded through the cornfields. They watched and smelled the smoke rising from the burning buildings and fields. They heard the axes chopping down their orchards. Their storehouses of corn were burning. The town of Tah-skee-gee was burning. Sequoyah's heart pounded. Around him he heard soft sobbing. He could see the pain and fear in people's eyes. He could feel the anger rising inside himself. But there was nothing he, nor anyone else, could do. They must wait. They must be patient. They must try to survive in the mountains, fighting off starvation and disease until it would be safe to return. Then they could rebuild and replant.

Tah-skee-gee was one of fifty Cherokee towns destroyed by the American armies in 1776. The town chiefs arranged for peace, surrendering land in return for promises of respect for Cherokee boundaries. The promises were not kept. There was more fighting between the Cherokees and the settlers. Four years later, mounted riflemen came back to the Little Tennessee River and destroyed the towns again. They burned over one thousand houses. This time even the peace capital, Echota, was leveled.

Many Cherokees became refugees during those violent years, fleeing to safety in distant places. The Cherokee settlement of Willstown, on the Coosa River in present-day Alabama, drew many of those refugees. Sequoyah was a young man when he and Wuh-teh packed their belongings and journeyed southwest to make a new home in Willstown.

Sequoyah helped his mother set up a successful trading business in Willstown. Each year they bought a supply of items—firearms, axes, knives, and hoes, as well as imported fabrics and beads. Cherokee farmers and hunters had come to rely on the metal tools and guns that had been introduced by European settlers. European-made fabrics had also become popular. The men continued to wear deerskin leggings and moccasins, but they also used cloth to create a distinctive style of dress—with patterned headdresses wrapped like turbans, loose-fitting hunting shirts, and knee-length outer garments. Decoration had always been a feature of Cherokee dress, and women had always embellished clothing with designs. But glass beads imported from Europe had now also been adopted, and the embroiderers quickly became adept at decorative beadwork.

Sequoyah and his mother exchanged their goods for deerskins and other furs supplied by Cherokee hunters. They then used the pelts to buy new supplies.

Sequoyah often accompanied the hunters on their expeditions.

He brought horses with him and gradually loaded them with the pelts that the hunters gave him. He, too, used those weeks in the woods to hunt for meat and skins. Then he returned to the trading house with his loaded horses.

Trading and hunting were not Sequoyah's only activities. He was still pursuing his interest in art. In the years since childhood, he had become more and more skilled. Always looking for ways to improve his drawings and paintings, he mixed new colors by using scrapings from tree barks and dyes from boiled berries and plants. He experimented with brushes of different thicknesses by using hairs from different animals. He often made his sketches on sheets of bark or paper. He painted on canvases he had made himself by treating animal skins. His subjects were usually the animals that had been part of his life since his boyhood in the mountains—deer, buffalo, hogs, horses.

Sequoyah's talents were becoming well known. Many people came to admire his work. One friend was so impressed by Sequoyah's sketches that he asked for lessons. Sequoyah was glad to share what he had learned. Years later a white man who had seen some of Sequoyah's paintings observed that "no man in the United States can surpass him in drawing a buffalo."

It was as a craftsman, however, that Sequoyah established his reputation. He taught himself the art of the silversmith. Silver items were much in demand among the Cherokees, who appreciated finely made jewelry and utensils. Sequoyah melted down the silver coins he had been given by European and American trappers and traders. He created silver spurs and spoons. He made ornamental buckles and plates for the harnesses of horses. Men and women alike wore jewelry, and Sequoyah's silver earrings, armlets, bracelets, and nose rings were known for their high quality.

Working with silver required patience. Sequoyah tried out various designs as he worked on each piece. There was always something he could do to make it even better, even more beautiful. Sequoyah knew that his silver work was superior. It seemed a shame that when an item left his shop, no one would know who had created it. The problem could be solved easily enough: Sequoyah could sign his work with his name.

The name *Sequoyah* was Cherokee, however, and everyone knew that the sounds of Cherokee words could not be written down accurately. But Sequoyah, like most Cherokees, had more than one name. Many people had an English name, which they used in dealings with whites. Sequoyah's English name was George Guess (or George Gist). It was based on his father's name, which was variously spelled *Guess* or *Gist* or *Guyst* or *Guest*. *George Guess* was the name that Sequoyah decided to stamp on his silver work.

Although Sequoyah could pronounce his English name, he spoke no English. And he could not write in any language. But there was a neighbor and friend, Charles Hicks, who could help him. Charles Hicks, who was later to become a principal chief of the Cherokee Nation, had been educated by missionaries who had come to the Nation in 1801. Sequoyah asked him for help. Hicks demonstrated how to shape the letters of the name *George Guess*. By copying each shape, Sequoyah created a stamp for his handiwork.

During these years, Sequoyah married a woman named U-ti-yu and started a family. He and U-ti-yu would have at least one son and one daughter.

When Wuh-teh died, sometime in the early 1800's, Sequoyah must have known how proud she was of the man he had become. A Cherokee account written in Sequoyah's own lifetime noted that the people who knew Sequoyah in those times "thought him a man of genius, capable of any thing he should choose to undertake."

After his mother's death, Sequoyah took over ownership of the trading house. It also served as a meeting place, and Sequoyah often played the role of generous host to friends and neighbors who gathered there. Everyone knew and liked Sequoyah; he was a charming, mild-mannered man. He took pleasure in his popularity and in the companionship of others. There were so many things to talk and laugh about. The hours passed easily and happily.

Because he was a trader, Sequoyah had access to something that could make these social occasions livelier—whiskey. He began to offer drinks to his friends. Then he began to drink himself.

To those who shared whiskey with Sequoyah, there was something comical at first about the effects that drinking had on him. He was a wonderful storyteller. And when liquor loosened his tongue, his stories could be hilarious. He sang songs, too, and made the young men laugh until he dozed off.

But whiskey's effects were not truly amusing, for Sequoyah was also neglecting his work. He began to drink too much too often. In the community, he was earning a new name, a shameful one: Drunken Sequoyah.

Sequoyah knew about the name. Drunken Sequoyah. In sober moments, he asked himself how this terrible thing had happened to him. How had he changed from a respected man into a drunk? He had seen other men drunk and knew how pitiful they looked. Women too. Drink was hard to resist, since the people loved to enjoy themselves and the effects of alcohol were so pleasant. But whiskey also took away the senses and made people do dishonorable things. At ball plays and other gatherings, Sequoyah saw vicious fights between spectators. This was not the Cherokee way. All people should get along with one another; that was the Cherokee way. Sequoyah knew that whiskey was destroying what was valuable to the Cherokees. He knew that whiskey was destroying him, too.

Sequoyah looked at himself and saw a man who had become useless. He was no longer a responsible husband and father. His need for whiskey held him like a trapped animal. It tormented him. He knew that he had to break free from the hold that alcohol had on him.

Sequoyah set himself to restoring the feelings that had meant so much to him as a boy attending the Green Corn ceremonies—the feelings of hopefulness and renewal. There was always hope. There was always a chance to start again on a better path. To set off on that path, Sequoyah called on two of the qualities that had helped him in his life so far—patience and persistence. He may also have sought support from others. Perhaps he approached Charles Hicks, who was embracing the whites' religion of Christianity and might offer comfort and understanding. Perhaps he went to Ah-gee-lee, his cousin and lifelong friend, asking for strength and help.

Somehow, Sequoyah succeeded. He never touched whiskey again. His experience made him try to persuade others to avoid drinking entirely. Eventually an anti-alcohol policy would be established throughout the Cherokee Nation.

# *Three*
# The Idea

With a fresh sense of purpose, Sequoyah took up a new trade. He became a blacksmith. Iron tools had been brought to Cherokee country by traders, and many people were using the new equipment. Sequoyah realized that more blacksmiths would be needed to repair those tools and make new ones. He had seen blacksmiths at work. Now he decided to teach himself the craft.

Sequoyah figured out how to build a forge and bellows. He made the drills, hammers, tongs, and other equipment that he needed to run his shop. He taught himself to repair hoes and axes, to sharpen plows, and to make knives. He made spurs and bridle bits, sometimes adding patterns of inlaid silver.

People traveled long distances to come to Sequoyah's shop, and he had many customers. Not all could pay right away, so Sequoyah offered them credit. Customers who owed him money would pay when they had it. But Sequoyah soon realized that his memory was not up to the task of recalling all the various amounts owed by different people. To solve the problem of tracking his customers' credits, Sequoyah devised an accounting method. He drew a simple picture to represent each customer. Beside it he drew a series of circles or lines, some of different sizes, representing the amount each person owed. This picture-and-symbol system turned out to be more accurate than memory.

One day Sequoyah was among a group of men who had gathered to talk and pass the time. The conversation turned to the peculiar talents of white people, including the ability to write messages. The Cherokees had often seen white soldiers, traders, and missionaries writing and reading. They had seen the English language recorded on paper in treaties, and they had seen the written accounts of traders, which told of Cherokee purchases and debts. They had to be told what these messages said. But a white person could understand a message that another white person, far away, had put down days or weeks before.

The Cherokee language had no word for "writing," since Cherokee speech had never been written down. The people referred to the messages on paper as "talking leaves."

The question that the Cherokee men were discussing was this: Did white people invent talking leaves by themselves, or did they receive that power as a gift from the Creator? Many Cherokees accepted the second alternative. There was even a popular story that offered an explanation. It was said that the first man on earth—an Indian—had received a book as a gift and was told to use it wisely. But while that man wasn't looking, a white man came along and stole the book, leaving a bow and arrow in its place.

Sequoyah listened as one man voiced the opinion that white people had many things that had not been granted to others. Several listeners agreed. Talking leaves were just one more example of a special gift that was not within the grasp of the Cherokees. It had to do with an unusual aspect of the mind, someone noted. It was a form of magic, said another.

Sequoyah had heard this kind of talk before, and he scoffed at it. He listened this time to the speakers' ideas and finally told them they were being foolish. "The white man is no magician," Sequoyah explained as he picked up a stone and a pin. He etched some marks on the stone and held it up, announcing that he had created a message. To understand such a message, he said, all that was needed was for the sender and the receiver to agree ahead of time what the marks meant.

Sequoyah's listeners burst out laughing. If you need to agree in advance what the marks mean, then why not just speak the message? Why bother writing it down? The idea of stones that could talk was plainly ridiculous.

The men began to mock Sequoyah. Talking stones! These will make poor company for you, they teased. Sequoyah was quiet. It was as if he did not even hear their ridicule. His mind had turned inward. He was thinking of a problem that needed solving. When he left, he said simply, "I know that I can make marks which can be understood."

It was clear to Sequoyah that the men had not understood what he meant. But what exactly *had* he meant? He had no doubt that Cherokee speech could be captured with marks on paper. But how could it be done?

Sequoyah awoke one morning aware of a pain in the knee of his weakened leg. Over the next several days, the pain grew stronger. It was as if a small creature were chewing on his knee. Sequoyah worked at his shop, trying to distance himself from the gnawing pain. When he decided it was time to rest, he tried to walk back to his cabin. His leg collapsed under him. Sequoyah could not stand.

He was brought home. His knee had swelled, and the skin around it was taut and tender. It looked fiery and felt hot to the touch. Sequoyah lay in bed. He felt as if he were burning up. Then he shivered with cold.

His family called for a healer, who recited chants to make the evil leave Sequoyah's body. The healer also made scratches on the swollen leg and rubbed the bleeding parts with a warm liquid made from specially selected plants. Sequoyah was taken into the *oh-see*, the hothouse, to lie beside the steaming rocks. When he crawled out from the earth-covered log house, his skin heated and dripping, the healer brought him to a cold stream, where he was plunged into the water.

Days passed. The healer returned with more chants and medicine and treatments. Sequoyah lay on his beaverskin mattress, unaware of what was happening around him, too weak to rise.

Eventually his fever broke. Some strength returned, and Sequoyah was well enough to sit up. But he would not be able to stand on his own for weeks.

Sequoyah spent day after day in the dim cabin, its only light coming through the open door. He had nothing to do but think. His ideas moved slowly, and he looked at them with care.

He recalled a hunting trip he had been on as a young man. He was with his cousin Ah-gee-lee and several other Cherokee hunters, and they came upon a group of white hunters. The white men were friendly. That night the two parties camped near each other. Ah-gee-lee, whose English name was George Lowrey, could speak a little English. He talked with the white men. One of the white hunters—he called himself Dickey—was especially talkative. He persuaded the Cherokees to tell him about their customs. Then he talked about his own way of life. He showed them a small book and explained what it contained. Afterward Sequoyah and Ah-gee-lee talked with enthusiasm about that book.

Now Sequoyah thought again about that time he had seen the white people's talking leaves. He thought about the many other useful things that white people had developed. His mother had made a business of trading iron tools and other items furnished by

Sequoyah's cousin and friend Ah-gee-lee. His English name was George Lowrey. The portrait shows the nose ring and earrings worn by some Cherokee men. Lowrey became an important leader of the Cherokee Nation, and was referred to by whites as the Cherokees' George Washington.

the whites. She had raised dairy cattle, even though cows and milk products were not originally Cherokee. She had shown him that it was often worthwhile to accept new ideas. The Cherokees had made good use of gifts from others, Sequoyah decided.

Changes seemed to be occurring rapidly now in the Nation. Many people were raising cattle and hogs for sale. They were hunting less and farming more. There were spinning wheels and looms in Cherokee cabins. Women were making clothing not only out of skins but also out of cotton and wool.

Years before, the leaders of the Cherokees had signed a treaty with George Washington, the leader of the new American nation. They had agreed with Washington that the future of the Cherokees depended on the people's adopting the ways of white civilization.

Sequoyah thought about these changes. Were they all good? Whiskey was a white invention, and it brought sorrow. Some Cherokee families were exchanging the old values for new ones. They were collecting wealth for themselves. They lived in two-story houses and sent their children away from Cherokee country to be educated like whites.

Lately young Cherokees had begun to abandon the old spiritual beliefs and adopt the Christian ideas taught by the missionaries. They were learning English, too. Sequoyah did not have much need for English. He did little business with English-speaking settlers, and when he did, he spoke the trade language shared by many peoples of the region. But young Cherokees were learning English not only to speak it with the whites, but also so that they could read and write.

Why should the Cherokee people have to abandon their language in order to use talking leaves? Sequoyah wondered. It seemed wrong and unnecessary. What would become of the people if they gave up their language? They would become separated from themselves, from what it meant to be Cherokee. Sequoyah thought about his beautiful language—its sounds flowing into one another like the breathing of a forest or the singing of a mountain stream. This was the language of loving parents, of powerful leaders, of brothers, sisters, cousins, friends, and of ancestors going all the way back through time—it was the heart of the people. It was the strongest tie the people had with one another and with their past.

Suddenly the Cherokee language seemed the most precious thing that Sequoyah could think of. It would never be lost if it could be preserved in writing. If the people could learn to write down their messages, their important speeches, and their history—all in their own beloved language—then their wisdom could be preserved for all time. No one would forget exactly what was said, as sometimes happened with spoken words.

If talking leaves could be made to speak Cherokee, then it would not be necessary to depend on English for reading and writing.

The idea of writing was an idea worth borrowing, if it could be made to fit Cherokee purposes. Sequoyah had discovered a new challenge. He had a new goal.

When Sequoyah recovered his health, he went back to his smithy. As he worked, he began to pay close attention to the sounds around him. He looked up thoughtfully when he heard the grunting of hogs and the cackling of chickens. He listened to the twittering of songbirds. There were barks and growls to turn an ear to. There was the laughter of people and their calls to one another. Quiet talk. Chants and songs.

Since childhood Sequoyah had been alert to the sounds of the forest. Now he seemed to be hearing them in new ways. He squinted at the darkness when the hooting of owls and other night noises floated through the air. It was said that such night sounds were the calls of witches and ghosts. Sequoyah listened and pondered. How could all those things be turned into permanent marks?

Fixing sounds on paper seemed, as he would later say, "like catching a wild animal and taming it."

He began his explorations in a way that was natural for an artist. He drew pictures. It seemed to make sense to use drawings to represent spoken ideas. A picture of a bird could mean "bird," and if it were shown flying, it could mean "flying bird." The same could be done with a galloping horse or a turtle on a log. But what if the bird was "a raven that flew overhead yesterday morning," or the horse "the spotted mare that my neighbor plans to sell to me"? There had to be a way to show each of those more complicated ideas with pictures, too. Sequoyah intended to figure out the way.

# *Four*
# The Pursuit

For the next several years, Sequoyah went on with his work as a blacksmith and a trader. He also went on with his work on a writing system. He listened, he thought, and he drew. In 1813 his efforts were interrupted. A call to duty had come from The Ridge, a Cherokee leader of great influence. (The Ridge had earned his name by the clearsighted nature of his decisions—he seemed to see things from on high, like someone standing on the ridge of a mountain.) The Ridge had been instructed by the Nation's principal chief, Pathkiller, to gather up Cherokee troops. These soldiers were to help Andrew Jackson, the general of the Tennessee militia. Jackson was leading the war against the Red Sticks, an anti–U.S. faction of the Creeks. Among those called to fight with Jackson and his army troops and militias were Cherokee, Chickasaw, Choctaw, and pro–U.S. Creek warriors.

Although Sequoyah was neither young nor fully able-bodied, he volunteered. He became a private in the company of Mounted and Foot Cherokees, which was part of a five-hundred-man force—the Regiment of Cherokee Indians. Sequoyah served for three months, participating in the surprise capture of a Creek town. A few weeks later, he reenlisted. On March 27, 1814, his regiment took part in the famous and dreadful Battle of the Horseshoe.

The Creeks had prepared for a last stand on a horseshoe-shaped peninsula on the Tallapoosa River in Alabama. They had built a log barricade for protection. Behind it was their encampment, with about one thousand warriors and three hundred women and children. And behind their houses were canoes moored to the riverbank, ready if retreat became necessary.

The Cherokee troops, distinguished by headdresses of white feathers and deer tails, had crossed the river about three miles downstream. They had then made their way back to positions behind the Creek encampment to prevent retreat. As Jackson bombarded the barricade with shot from two small cannons, several Cherokees swam to the Creek canoes. They used the canoes to ferry their own men to the rear of the Creek camp. Surprised, the Creeks at the barricades dropped their defenses, and Jackson's troops swarmed into the camp. What followed was the largest Indian battle in the history of the United States.

The fighting was close and bloody. When more than half the Creek warriors lay shot, bayoneted, or tomahawked, the others attempted retreat. They were killed at the river's edge or in the water. The Battle of the Horseshoe was a massacre, for almost all

This portrait of The Ridge was made in 1834.

the Creek men, women, and children were killed. The Red Sticks' resistance was broken, and the Creek War was over.

Called Sharp Knife by the Cherokees and Old Hickory by the Americans, Andrew Jackson was a tough warrior who was destined to become president of the United States. The Battle of the Horseshoe made him famous. But he would forget that he owed a debt to the Cherokees for making his victory possible.

It is not known if Sequoyah participated in the canoe-stealing operation or in the deadly combat, or if he served in another way—guarding provisions or horses, perhaps. He was discharged fifteen days after the battle. As he rode back to his home, he and other Cherokee veterans found that their lands were not as they had left them. American troops had devastated Cherokee farms, not just to feed themselves but for the sake of destruction, it seemed. Hogs had been slaughtered and crops destroyed. The Cherokee leadership protested, but it took two years before the United States government agreed to pay the Nation for the damage that had been done to Cherokee property.

When the Cherokee delegates were in Washington arranging payment for their wartime losses, they also signed two treaties in which they gave up land. The land included their last strip of South Carolina territory. These land-ceding treaties were not the first ones the Cherokees had signed, and they would not be the last. The Cherokees were overwhelmingly outnumbered. There

Andrew Jackson, painted about 1815.

were about one million American settlers in the southeastern states, surrounding only thirteen thousand Cherokees. The settlers wanted land, and the Cherokees had it.

The Cherokee National Council was aware that the Americans often used bribery and threats to force representatives to sign away land. The Council wanted to make sure that Cherokee representatives would not make land deals. Soon it would pass a law pronouncing the death penalty on any Cherokees who signed such agreements without the Nation's consent.

In 1816 Sequoyah was selected to be one of the delegates to the Chickasaw Council House, where Andrew Jackson hoped to have yet another land-ceding treaty signed. The fifteen Cherokee delegates were given strict orders: "Sell no land."

At the meeting, Sequoyah listened to the arguments that Jackson made through an interpreter. The United States government was interested in the welfare of the Cherokees, Jackson explained. But the government could not protect the people from white settlers who would be coming in ever greater numbers to settle in Cherokee territories. Look to your future safety, Jackson and the other American commissioners advised the Cherokees. Think about your children and grandchildren. Just give up Cherokee claims to this one area—3,500 square miles in Alabama—and the United States government will pay six thousand dollars a year for ten years to the Cherokee Nation. And any Cherokees who abandon their farms and homes in this region will be paid for them. The Cherokees could still claim their homelands north of the Tennessee River.

Sequoyah and the other delegates listened silently. They talked among themselves. They had not needed to be told to think about their children and grandchildren—they had always assumed that the generations of the future were their responsibility.

It was true that game was beginning to disappear from the regions of white settlement. It was becoming harder to lead the life of a Cherokee hunter. Perhaps by giving up this land, the Cherokees would be safeguarding their other lands. But could they trust the Americans? Did they even have a choice? Jackson was clearly a powerful man, and a determined one.

The delegates knew that they had no authority to sign away land. That is why they insisted that the treaty not be binding until the National Council approved it. With that condition understood, twelve of the delegates signed. Sequoyah took his turn, marking his X next to the name George Guess.

Jackson still had to persuade the Nation's leaders to sign. At the National Council later that year, he managed to do just that, and even Chief Pathkiller signed the treaty.

Sequoyah's selection as a delegate to an important meeting showed that he was well respected in the Cherokee community. When his wartime service ended in 1814, he had returned to Willstown. A year later he married for the second time. (His first marriage had ended, probably by simple agreement. Divorce was not unusual among the Cherokees.) Sequoyah's new wife was a young woman named Sally, and she came from a well-known and prosperous Cherokee family.

Despite his growing responsibilities as husband and father, Sequoyah found himself more and more preoccupied with his pursuit of a writing system. He was always listening, continually drawing.

He had already given up on the notion of making pictures to represent complete ideas. That system was too complicated, and it would require every writer to have artistic talent. It made more sense to use symbols, or characters, to represent smaller units of meaning. When put together, the characters could express bigger ideas.

Sequoyah made several visits to the mission school at Spring Place. He watched and listened as the children learned to read from English books. A teacher gave him a copy of a spelling book to take with him. Sequoyah examined the symbols, and he practiced copying them. It was easy enough to draw these characters, and it was also easy to invent new ones. The hard part was knowing what to say when seeing one of the characters. There seemed to be so many different words in the Cherokee language. Would every one of them need to be shown with a different character or combination of characters? Sequoyah thought so, even though that meant hundreds—no, tens of hundreds—of characters.

The work was important. It took time, too, and concentration. Sequoyah built himself a small cabin apart from his family. There he would sit for hours, pulling on his long pipe and pausing to mutter a word or phrase. *The fox is barking*—had he a character for fox and for the sound of the fox? *The sky is filling with water*—what about sky, rain, what about swollen clouds? Did he have characters for all those things? Sequoyah was patient. He filled page after page with patterns of marks. When he ran out of paper, he wrote his characters on wood shingles. He would look at each set of marks and ask himself, Do I remember what this says? And he would repeat the words aloud.

Sequoyah found that he was barely able to hold a normal conversation anymore. When people spoke to him, he listened not so much to what they were saying but to how they were saying it. And while he appeared to be listening, he was often thinking, Do I have a character for that idea? Or, What characters make up that saying?

The time came when Sequoyah was spending days alone in his cabin. He was no longer working at the blacksmith trade, no longer helping to look after the family's crops. Sally was taking care of everything herself—the vegetables, the hogs, the housekeeping, the children. One day a hunter came by to tell Sally that he had seen Sequoyah in the woods. He described Sequoyah sitting on the ground and playing like a child with chips of wood. Sequoyah did not even lift his head when the hunter called out to him. He was so absorbed in his play, the hunter said, that he did not hear the call.

Sally was growing ever more annoyed at her husband. In her eyes, Sequoyah had become lazy and irresponsible. She was also worried. What Sequoyah was doing was unnatural. Many of the neighbors, aware of Sequoyah's odd and incessant mutterings, watched the weeds overgrow his land and suspected witchcraft. The penalty for such evil doings was death.

Sequoyah's friend Turtle Fields came to him to tell of the gossip spreading in the community. "Our people are very concerned about you," Turtle Fields said. "They think you are wasting your life. They think, my friend, that you are making a fool of yourself, and will no longer be respected."

Sequoyah had always valued the respect of others. But somehow this pursuit of symbols that spoke seemed more important than anything else. More important, even, than what others thought of him. He tried to explain to Turtle Fields that this was a matter of a personal choice. "What I have done I have done by myself. If our people think I am making a fool of myself, tell them that what I am doing will not make fools of them." Sequoyah was sure of himself. "They did not make me begin, and they shall not make me give up. If I am no longer respected, what I am doing will not make our people less respected, either by themselves or others. So I shall go on," he said definitely. "And that is what you may tell our people."

Turtle Fields did not argue further. But Sally, along with several fearful neighbors, decided to put a stop to Sequoyah's strange pastime. Suppose he really were possessed by evil spirits? It was in Sequoyah's own interest that he be discouraged from this dangerous activity. The neighbors waited for Sally's signal that her husband had left his cabin. Then they went in and set it ablaze. All the pages and wood chips covered with symbols—all the years of thought and labor—turned to ash.

Sequoyah returned in time to watch the smoke rising from the embers. He surveyed the destruction and trembled. Why had he not been allowed to do his work? Why did others have to interfere? What was he left with now? Nothing. Nothing but this terrible loss and heartbreaking disappointment.

But even as he thought about all that was lost, Sequoyah stirred up new possibilities. He had always believed in being hopeful. His patience had always been rewarded. It was not long before Sequoyah was able to think about starting over. As he considered the work he had done, he knew he could reconstruct much of it. But perhaps reconstruction was not the answer.

Perhaps this fire was a good thing. Perhaps he had been on the wrong path and needed to begin again anyway. Yes, it was time to try a different approach to writing the Cherokee language. It was time to toss out old ideas and start over. A new plan began to take vague shape in Sequoyah's mind.

# Five
# It Works

Sequoyah decided to pursue his new plan elsewhere, by becoming one of the Arkansas Emigrants.

It was 1818. As a result of another land-ceding treaty with Andrew Jackson in 1817, volunteers were being asked to give up their property in exchange for lands to the west, in the Arkansas Territory. Arkansas had been home for about ten years to a group of Cherokee emigrants known as the Old Settlers. Now their leader, Oo-loo-deh-gah (whose English name was John Jolly), persuaded other Eastern Cherokees to join the Old Settlers. Sequoyah signed up.

Sequoyah joined more than three hundred emigrants in a river journey that took seventy days. In thirteen flatboats and four keelboats, the people sat amid their few possessions and watched the shores slip by—the Tennessee River, the Ohio River, the great Mississippi. Then they boarded a steamboat up the Arkansas River to their destination, fertile wilderness on the north side of the Arkansas, in what is today Pope County.

Here Sequoyah built himself a home. Here he continued to study the Cherokee language. He listened closely as his friends and neighbors spoke. And here it came to him that a writing system need not depend on symbols standing for meanings. Symbols could stand for *sounds*! Sequoyah felt the thrill of a solution just within reach. The characters he drew would stand not for sentences or phrases or words, but for the *parts* within those utterances. Once Sequoyah understood that the same sounds were put together in different ways in all the words that the people ever spoke, he had the key he needed. He knew he could unlock the mystery of written Cherokee.

Sequoyah worked purposefully. He listened. As people pronounced words, he heard the patterns of sounds repeated within them. He detected the syllables that make up the Cherokee language. Sequoyah heard syllables like these (here written in the Roman alphabet used for English):

lah lay lee loh loo
hah hay hee hoh hoo
tsah tsay tsee tsoh tsoo
sah say see soh soo
tlah tlay tlee tloh tloo

These examples are only approximations of the sounds of Cherokee. The missionaries who had come to the Nation were trying to use the Roman alphabet to write the Cherokee language, but they were finding it frustrating. The Cherokee language has sounds that do not occur in English, so it is difficult to match them with English spellings. The Cherokee sound that is often spelled *ts*, for example, is actually pronounced somewhere between *ts*, *ch*, and *j* by Cherokee speakers. There are other Cherokee sounds that are difficult to capture. The name *Cherokee* itself illustrates the problem: It is also written *Tsa-la-gi*.

But Sequoyah was not burdened by knowledge of English and its Roman alphabet. Free to listen to his own familiar language, he heard its syllables and the sounds within them. He detected the small rush of breath that accompanied some of the sounds, and the *unh,* like a small grunt, that was a part of many words.

He heard more than two hundred different syllables and drew a symbol for each one. His characters were his own creations, made of complex, swirling strokes.

When Sequoyah spoke in sequence the sounds that the characters symbolized, their meaning leaped off the page. Sequoyah knew he had done it.

When Sequoyah left Arkansas to visit the Cherokee Nation back east, he carried with him precious papers containing the not-yet-final list of syllables. He also had written messages from Old Settlers to their friends and relatives in the Nation. Sequoyah delivered the messages in person, reading them aloud from the page.

The people were glad to get word from their loved ones so far away. Some were startled to see Sequoyah reading the Cherokee language from pieces of paper. But none could believe that the leaves were talking in Cherokee. They assumed that Sequoyah had memorized the messages. Memorizing was, after all, the method that everyone had always used to preserve speech.

It was 1821. Sequoyah was putting in place the last pieces of the language puzzle. He had worked on reducing two hundred different characters to a more manageable 86 (which would later be simplified to 85). Many of the characters now resembled shapes he had seen in English print. Sequoyah's 86-character syllabary could spell all the Cherokee words anyone could ever think of. A syllabary is a kind of alphabet in which each character stands for a syllable. To send a message, all anyone would have to do was pronounce each word somewhat slowly and write the character that stood for each syllable. If Sequoyah wrote, for example, ᎠᏆᏂᏔ the symbols would speak the syllables—*ah-QUAH-nee-tah*. And the meaning—"I know"—would come clear. The only task left—and it was a formidable one—was convincing people that the system worked.

A syllabary is the ideal system for the Cherokee language, in which almost all syllables begin with a consonant sound and end with a vowel. A syllabary would not do for most English words, but the few listed below give a sense of how such a system works (pronounce each letter name to hear the word or words in parentheses):

| | |
|---|---|
| NME (enemy) | MT (empty) |
| EZ (easy) | ICU (I see you) |
| XPDNC (expediency) | RUOK? (Are you okay?) |

Sequoyah was sure of himself and satisfied with what he had done. In Willstown he made a visit to the home of his cousin Ah-gee-lee, who was now the town chief. Ah-gee-lee had heard about Sequoyah's writing and asked him how he was getting on.

"I am getting on very well," Sequoyah replied. "I can write down anything I have heard. I then put it aside. I take it up again days later and there find all that I heard exactly as I heard it."

"It may be that you are not forgetful," his cousin suggested. "Your understanding of the message may come not from the marks you have invented, but from what these marks lead you to remember." Perhaps the marks merely helped Sequoyah to form associations, like someone trained to interpret the patterns on a wampum belt. Such a person could make long memorized speeches based on what those patterns suggested.

"The same marks will make me remember very different things, according to the way in which I place them," Sequoyah said. He described how after he had written something he always put it aside and gave it no further thought. "I do not remember what I have written. But at any time afterward, I can pick up the paper and recall everything."

Ah-gee-lee remained skeptical. Soon afterward, when Ah-gee-lee was on a visit to Sequoyah's home, Sequoyah proudly called to his young daughter, Ah-yo-kah. She was a small child, perhaps as young as six. When she came to her father's side, he held a copy of his syllabary out to her and asked her to recite from it. Quickly—she had enjoyed playing this game with her father before—she pronounced the series of syllables. "Yah!" Ah-gee-lee exclaimed with astonishment. "It sounds like the Creek language."

"But the sounds, put together, make Cherokee words," Sequoyah explained. He then wrote out characters that Ah-yo-kah pronounced in sequence. She was speaking Cherokee words! Ah-gee-lee was amazed. But he was no longer doubtful. He had seen and heard for himself that Sequoyah's writing system worked.

Ah-yo-kah was one of Sequoyah's first pupils. She mastered the system easily. Sequoyah's brother-in-law was another early learner. Sequoyah's nephew learned, too. It was one thing to find relatives who would accept the syllabary, but quite another to win acceptance in the Nation.

It was when Sequoyah made a legal claim at Indian Court that others began to notice his achievement. Sequoyah came prepared with a written account of his case. When he read aloud from the page, in Cherokee, he was doing something that his listeners had never seen or heard before.

The next day a man called Big Rattling Gourd came to Sequoyah. He had witnessed Sequoyah's reading. "I could not sleep last night," Big Rattling Gourd said. "Yesterday by daylight what you did did not seem remarkable. But when night came, it was different. All night long I wondered at it and could not sleep."

Big Rattling Gourd had been kept awake by the sudden understanding of what Sequoyah's syllabary could do. It was something to marvel at. "This surpasses anything I ever thought possible for a man to accomplish," Big Rattling Gourd said.

Sequoyah explained that he had done it for a good purpose, even though everyone thought he was injuring himself and his family.

Big Rattling Gourd asked Sequoyah one question after another. "Can you write anything you choose? Or must it be only particular things?"

Sequoyah replied that he could write anything at all, provided it was spoken in Cherokee. "If it is in any other language, I cannot write it."

"I remember the chiefs of the past and the speeches they made. If I repeat those speeches to you, will you be able to write them down?" Big Rattling Gourd felt it was important that these speeches be recorded faithfully. At councils, speakers quoted from these speeches, but he knew that their quotations were not always accurate.

Sculpture *Sequoyah and Ahyokah* by Cherokee artist Bob Annesley.

Sequoyah explained that this was one of the uses of the syllabary. Anyone who had memory of an important speech or event could now find a way to preserve it for all time.

When Big Rattling Gourd left, his mind was filled with possibilities for this wondrous invention.

Acceptance was not widespread, however. One of the reasons was Sequoyah's lingering reputation as a worker of witchcraft. Many people of influence in the Nation still believed that Sequoyah's invention was something evil. He would have to prove that his syllabary was a powerful tool for the good of the people.

Sequoyah and Ah-yo-kah stood before a gathering of men and women to demonstrate how his invention worked. He pointed to a distant spot and told Ah-yo-kah to stand there, far out of hearing range. She walked away as instructed. Then Sequoyah asked someone to speak a message to him. He wrote the message on a piece of paper and handed it to one of the group. He motioned for Ah-yo-kah to return. Now I will walk off, he told the group, and Ah-yo-kah will speak the message by looking at the paper.

When he was gone, Ah-yo-kah looked at the characters her father had written. Calmly, she recited the syllables. The people looked at one another with wide eyes. The child had spoken the same words that her father had been told! How could this be?

Now someone told Ah-yo-kah a word. She wrote it down while Sequoyah stood in the distance. Then she walked off, and he returned to read aloud from the paper. He spoke the same word his daughter had been told!

But the people were still not convinced. It might be a trick of some kind, arranged in advance by father and child. It was witchcraft! Immediately there was talk that Sequoyah and Ah-yo-kah were working evil and would have to be executed.

Sequoyah held his small daughter beside him. Would his people never understand what he was offering them? The men and women were muttering now about the threat that Sequoyah and Ah-yo-kah posed to their community. Ah-gee-lee quieted them. He suggested that another test be given, one that could not be questioned.

Ah-gee-lee sent for several young men from other towns. Sequoyah met with them to train them in the use of the syllabary. The young men became eager learners when Sequoyah explained how his system worked. When their training was complete, they submitted themselves for a public test.

One at a time, each young man was brought into the Council house and told a message. Each wrote down his message, handed his paper to the Council leader, and left. The papers were shuffled, and the young men came back. Each was given a paper—different from the one he had written on—and took a turn reading its message aloud. The people in the Council house turned to one another with excitement: These were clearly the same messages that had been spoken earlier!

This was proof. The syllabary worked. It was not magic, it was not memorizing. It was writing. Sequoyah had given the Cherokee people their own talking leaves.

# Six
# The Results

Sequoyah had presented the talking leaves to his people, and at last they accepted his gift. It was one more contribution the Cherokee Nation would adopt in the name of progress. Literacy, the ability to read and write, would now belong to the Cherokees.

Reading and writing were practical skills. To be able to capture speech in writing and to send messages long distances were useful things. To be able to do those things in one's own language was also a matter of pride.

Sequoyah's syllabary became the talk of the Nation. Young and old practiced making the marks and pronouncing the sounds. With charcoal on bark, with the point of a stick on earth, with pen and paper, they could learn to build words in a day. A little more practice and memorizing, and they could record a message to be read back later. It was said that a learner could be reading and writing in just three days. Sequoyah's syllabary was that simple to use.

Not everyone was equally sensitive to the sounds of speech.

# Cherokee Alphabet.

| | | | | | |
|---|---|---|---|---|---|
| Ꭰ a | Ꭱ e | Ꭲ i | Ꭳ o | Ꭴ u | Ꭵ v |
| Ꭶ ga Ꭷ ka | Ꭸ ge | Ꭹ gi | Ꭺ go | Ꭻ gu | Ꭼ gv |
| Ꭽ ha | Ꭾ he | Ꭿ hi | Ꮀ ho | Ꮁ hu | Ꮂ hv |
| Ꮃ la | Ꮄ le | Ꮅ li | Ꮆ lo | Ꮇ lu | Ꮈ lv |
| Ꮉ ma | Ꮊ me | Ꮋ mi | Ꮌ mo | Ᏽ mu | |
| Ꮎ na Ꮏ hna Ꮐ nah | Ꮑ ne | Ꮒ ni | Ꮓ no | Ꮔ nu | Ꮕ nv |
| Ꮖ qua | Ꮗ que | Ꮘ qui | Ꮙ quo | Ꮚ quu | Ꮛ quv |
| Ꮜ sa Ꮝ s | Ꮞ se | Ꮟ si | Ꮠ so | Ꮡ su | Ꮢ sv |
| Ꮣ da Ꮤ ta | Ꮥ de Ꮦ te | Ꮧ di Ꮨ ti | Ꮩ do | Ꮪ du | Ꮫ dv |
| Ꮬ dla Ꮭ tla | Ꮮ tle | Ꮯ tli | Ꮰ tlo | Ꮱ tlu | Ꮲ tlv |
| Ꮳ tsa | Ꮴ tse | Ꮵ tsi | Ꮶ tso | Ꮷ tsu | Ꮸ tsv |
| Ꮹ wa | Ꮺ we | Ꮻ wi | Ꮼ wo | Ꮽ wu | Ꮾ wv |
| Ꮿ ya | Ᏸ ye | Ᏹ yi | Ᏺ yo | Ᏻ yu | Ᏼ yv |

## Sounds Represented by Vowels

a, as <u>a</u> in <u>father</u>, or short as <u>a</u> in <u>rival</u>

e, as <u>a</u> in <u>hate</u>, or short as <u>e</u> in <u>met</u>

i, as <u>i</u> in <u>pique</u>, or short as <u>i</u> in <u>pit</u>

o, as <u>o</u> in <u>note</u>, approaching <u>aw</u> in <u>law</u>

u, as <u>oo</u> in <u>fool</u>, or short as <u>u</u> in <u>pull</u>

v, as <u>u</u> in <u>but</u>, nasalized

## Consonant Sounds

<u>g</u> nearly as in English, but approaching to <u>k</u>. <u>d</u> nearly as in English but approaching to <u>t</u>. <u>h k l m n q s t w y</u> as in English. Syllables beginning with <u>g</u> except Ꭶ (ga) have sometimes the power of <u>k</u>. Ꭺ (go), Ꮪ (du), Ꮫ (dv) are sometimes sounded <u>to</u>, <u>tu</u>, <u>tv</u> and syllables written with tl except Ꮭ (tla) sometimes vary to dl.

This chart from a modern Cherokee language book is like those seen by nineteenth-century learners. It shows the symbol-syllable connections that Sequoyah devised.

Not everyone used exactly the same syllables to make the same words, so spelling was not uniform. But it did not matter. Someone receiving a message would pronounce each written character, and the combination of syllables would come close enough to spoken words to be immediately recognizable.

The people wanted to use the syllabary. A learner soon became a teacher, and new learners became new teachers. Literacy spread in this natural way, without desks or drills or schoolrooms. The Cherokees were the first Indian nation to become literate.

The people wrote letters to one another. It was possible now to send news-filled messages between family and friends in the east and in the Arkansas Territory. Sequoyah had returned with his family to Arkansas. There he was helping the other settlers to learn to use his syllabary.

It was possible now to keep records of Council meetings and to write notes to oneself about something that needed to be remembered. Even the healers adopted the syllabary. At last they could write down the centuries-old secret rituals that had been preserved only in memory. Now on paper they recorded the recipes and formulas for everything from curing disease to guaranteeing strength to finding lost items to keeping a husband and wife together. It would all be preserved.

The Christian missionaries in the Nation began to see that Sequoyah's syllabary had value for them, too. Some had been trying to adapt the Cherokee language to an English alphabet, but they

60

[illegible]

[illegible]

[illegible] XVII.

1 [illegible]

61

[illegible]

2 [illegible]

3 [illegible]

4 [illegible]

5 [illegible]

6 [illegible]

7 [illegible]

8 [illegible]

9 [illegible]

10 [illegible]

11 [illegible]

12 [illegible]

These pages come from a Cherokee hymn book published in 1888.

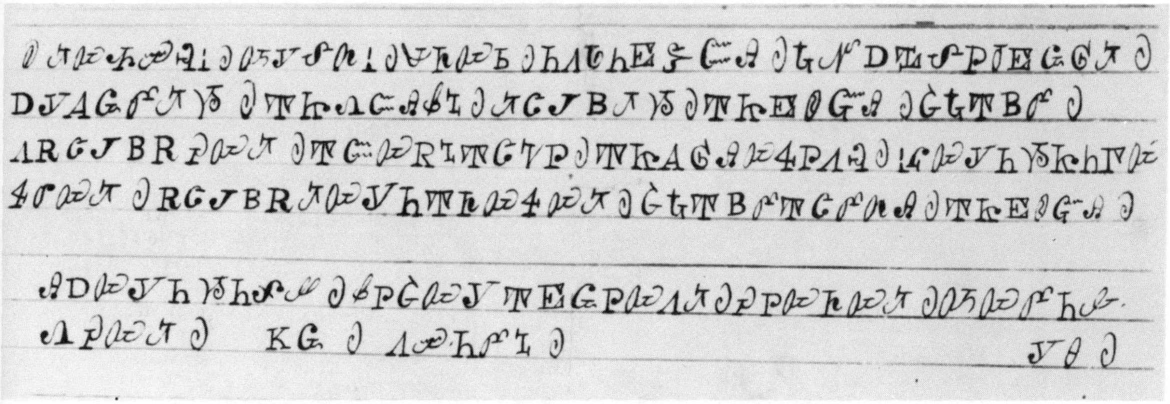

An example of a note written in the Cherokee syllabary. Some scholars believe it was written by Sequoyah himself.

gave up in favor of the syllabary, which was clearly more popular. The missionaries used the syllabary in their religious teachings and in their classrooms.

In 1824 a grateful National Council commissioned a silver medal to honor Sequoyah. Its inscription read, "Presented to George Gist by the General Council of the Cherokee Nation for his ingenuity in the invention of the Cherokee Alphabet: 1825." It was 1832 before the medal was taken west to be delivered to Sequoyah. The letter that accompanied it, signed by Chief John Ross, included the observation that "the present generation have already experienced the great benefits of your incomparable system." Sequoyah wore that medal for the rest of his life.

In 1825 the Cherokees in the east began to plan for a printing press. The Council voted to request donations that would enable them to purchase "two sets of types to fit one press . . . one set to

Elias Boudinot.

be composed of English letters, the other of Cherokee characters, the invention of George Guest, a Cherokee."

To find donors willing to make loans, a young Cherokee man who had taken the English name Elias Boudinot went on a speaking tour of the northern states. Boudinot had been educated at a mission school in New England. His English was faultless, and his manner was refined. He spoke of the progress of the Cherokees. His tour was a big success. Enough money came in to set in motion a plan for the press.

The characters of the syllabary needed to be cast in type. The type was made in Boston under the supervision of a missionary who had begun to live with the Cherokees, Samuel Worcester. Then the type and the parts for the press took a two-month journey by sea and land to New Echota, Georgia. A log house was built to hold the press and equipment. It took a while for the printing paper to arrive, but at last publishing began.

The press would produce many publications in the Cherokee language. The first book ever published in Cherokee was a fifty-page hymnal. There would be copies of the laws passed by the National Council, political pamphlets, religious publications, and notices warning of the evils of alcohol. But the most famous work of the press was a newspaper. For the first time in history, a newspaper appeared with articles written in an American Indian language.

On the masthead of the newspaper was its name: in Cherokee,

ᏣᎳᎩ ᏧᎴᎯᏌᏅᎯ (*Tsa-la-gi Tsu-le-hi-sa-nuh-hi*). The translation is "Cherokee will-rise-again"; in English the newspaper was called the *Cherokee Phoenix*, named for the bird of myth who rose up out of its own ashes to life.

Elias Boudinot became the editor of the *Phoenix*. "The great and sole motive in establishing this paper," Boudinot wrote, "is the benefit of the Cherokees." The newspaper was a four-page weekly. It published the laws and documents of the Nation, accounts of Cherokee progress, articles about other Indian peoples, interesting news of the day, correspondence from readers, editorials, and feature articles of general appeal.

Only about one third of the text was in Cherokee. The rest was in English. Cherokee readers who knew no English could subscribe to the paper free of charge. The publishers were eager for a native readership. But they wanted the *Phoenix* to circulate beyond the Nation, too. Cherokee leaders wanted Americans and Europeans to be aware of the Cherokees and their situation in Georgia, where they faced threats to their survival.

The newspaper did succeed in gaining attention. Readers as far away as New England and even Germany became subscribers.

The first issue of the *Phoenix* was dated February 21, 1828. In 1829 its name was changed to the *Cherokee Phoenix and Indians' Advocate*, with this motto: "Printed Under the Patronage, and for the Benefit of the Cherokee Nation, and Devoted to the Cause of the Indians."

PROTECTION

# ᏣᎳᎩ ᏧᎴᎯᏌᏅᎯ

# CHEROKEE PHŒNIX,

VOL. I. NEW ECHOTÁ, THURSDAY FEBRUARY 21, 1828. NO. 1.

EDITED BY ELIAS BOUDINOTT.

PRINTED WEEKLY BY

ISAAC H. HARRIS,

FOR THE CHEROKEE NATION.

At $2 50 if paid in advance, $3 in six months, or $3 50 if paid at the end of the year.

To subscribers who can read only the Cherokee language the price will be $2,00 in advance, or $2,50 to be paid within the year.

Every subscription will be considered as continued unless subscribers give notice to the contrary before the commencement of a new year.

The Phœnix will be printed on a Super-Royal sheet, with type entirely new procured for the purpose. Any person procuring six subscribers, and becoming responsible for the payment, shall receive a seventh gratis.

Advertisements will be inserted at seventy-five cents per square for the first insertion, and thirty-seven and a half cents for each continuance; longer ones in proportion.

☞All letters addressed to the Editor, post paid, will receive due attention.

[illegible]

## A GOOD CONSCIENCE.

What is there, in all the pomp of the world, the enjoyments of luxury, or the gratification of passion, comparable to the tranquil delight of a *good conscience? It is the health of the mind.* It is a sweet perfume, that diffuses its fragrance over every thing near it without exhausting its store. Unaccompanied with this, the gay pleasures of the world are like brilliants to a diseased eye, music to a deaf ear, wine in an ardent fever, or dainties in the languor of an ague. To lie down on the pillow, after a day spent in temperance in beneficence, and piety, how sweet is it! How different from the state of him, who reclines, at an unnatural hour, with his blood inflamed, his head throbbing with wine and gluttony, his heart aching with rancorous malice, his thoughts totally estranged from Him who has protected him in the day, and will watch over him, ungrateful as he is, in the night season! A good conscience is, indeed, the peace of God. passions lulled to sleep, clear thoughts, cheerful temper, a disposition to be pleased with every obvious and innocent object around; these are the effects of a good conscience; these are the things which constitute happiness; and these condescend to dwell with the poor man, in his humble cottage in the vale of obscurity. In the magnificent mansion of the proud and vain, glitter the exteriors of happiness, the gilding, the trapping, the pride, and the pomp; but in the decent habitation of piety is oftener found the downy nest of heavenly peace; that solid *good*, of which the parade of the vain, the frivolous, and voluptuous, is but a shadowy semblance.

*Christian Philosophy.*

*Flattery.*—Few things are more universally condemned than flattery: yet there are few men, who are above its influence, and still fewer, who have courage sufficient to repel it with a faithful rebuke. The following anecdote is recommended, as affording a specimen of a good answer to flatterers. A certain clergyman in New England, eminent both for talents and humility, was one day accosted by a parishioner, who highly commended some of his performances, of which the clergyman himself had a very low opinion. After patiently hearing him a few moments, the clergyman replied; "My Friend, all that you say gives me no better opinion of myself than I had before, but gives me a much worse opinion of you."

## CONSTITUTION OF THE CHEROKEE NATION,

*Formed by a Convention of Delegates from the several Districts, at New Echota, July* 1827.

We, the Representatives of the people of the Cherokee Nation in Convention assembled, in order to establish justice, ensure tranquility, promote our common welfare, and secure to ourselves and our posterity the blessings of liberty; acknowledging with humility and gratitude the goodness of the sovereign Ruler of the Universe, in offering us an opportunity so favorable to the design, and imploring his aid and direction in its accomplishment, do ordain and establish this Constitution for the Government of the Cherokee Nation.

### Article I.

Sec. 1. The Boundaries of this nation, embracing the lands solemnly guarantied and reserved forever to the Cherokee Nation by the Treaties concluded with the United States, are as follows; and shall forever hereafter remain unalterably the same—to wit—Beginning on the North Bank of Tennessee River at the upper part of the Chickasaw old fields; thence along the main channel of said river, including all the islands therein, to the mouth of the Hiwassee river, thence up the main channel of said river, including Islands, to the first hill which closes in on said river, about two miles above Hiwassee old Town; thence along the ridge which divides the waters of the Hiwassee and little Tellico, to the Tennessee river at Tallassee; thence along the main channel, including Islands, to the junction of the Cowee and Nanteyalee; thence along the ridge in the fork of said river, to the top of the blue ridge; thence along the blue ridge to the Unicoy Turnpike road; thence by a straight line to the main source of the Chestatee; thence along its main channel, including Islands, to the Chattahoochy; and thence down the same to the Creek boundary at Buzzard Roost; thence along the boundary line which separates this and the Creek Nation, to a point on the Coosa river opposite the mouth of Wills Creek; thence down along the South bank of the same to a point opposite to Fort Strother; thence up the river to the mouth of Wills Creek; thence up along the East bank of said creek, to the West branch thereof, and up the same to its source; and thence along the ridge which separates the Tombechee and Tennessee waters, to a point on the top of said ridge; thence due North to Camp Coffee on Tennessee river, which is opposite the Chickasaw Island; thence to the place of beginning.

Sec. 2. The Sovereignty and Jurisdiction of this Government shall extend over the Country within the boundaries above described, and the lands therein are, and shall remain, the common property of the Nation; but the improvements made thereon, and in the possession of the citizens of the Nation, are the exclusive and indefeasible property of the citizens respectively who made, or may rightfully be in possession of them; *Provided*, That the citizens of the Nation, possessing exclusive and indefeasible right to their respective improvements, as expressed in this article, shall possess no right nor power to dispose of their improvements in any manner whatever to the United States, individual States, nor to individual citizens thereof; and that, whenever any such citizen or citizens shall remove with their effects out of the limits of this Nation, and become citizens of any other Government, all their rights and privileges as citizens of this Nation shall cease; *Provided nevertheless*, That the Legislature shall have power to re-admit by law to all the rights of citizenship, any such person or persons, who may at any time desire to return to the Nation on their memorializing the General Council for such readmission. *Moreover*, the Legislature shall have power to adopt such laws and regulations, as its wisdom may deem expedient and proper, to prevent the citizens from monopolizing improvements with the view of speculation.

### Article II.

Sec. 1. The Power of this Government shall be divided into three distinct departments;—the Legislative, the Executive, and the Judicial.

Sec. 2. No person or persons, belonging to one of these Departments, shall exercise any of the powers properly belonging to either of the others, except in the cases hereinafter expressly directed or permitted.

### Article III.

Sec. 1. The Legislative Power shall be vested in two distinct branches; a Committee, and a Council; each to have a negative on the other, and both to be styled, the General Council of the Cherokee Nation; and the style of their acts and laws shall be,

"Resolved by the Committee and Council in General Council convened."

Sec. 2. The Cherokee Nation, as laid off into eight Districts, shall so remain.

Sec. 3. The Committee shall consist of two members from each District, and the Council shall consist of three members from each District, to be chosen by the qualified electors of their respective Districts for two years; and the elections to be held in every District on the first Monday in August for the year 1828, and every succeeding two years thereafter; and the General Council shall be held once a year, to be convened on the second Monday of October in each year, at New Echota.

Sec. 4. No person shall be eligible to a seat in the General Council, but a free Cherokee Male citizen, who shall have attained to the age of twenty-five years. The descendants of Cherokee men by all free women, except the African race, whose parents may be or have been living together as man and wife, according to the customs and laws of this Nation, shall be entitled to all the rights and privileges of this Nation, as well as the posterity of Cherokee women by all free men. No person who is of negro or mulatto parentage, either by the father or mother side, shall be eligible to hold any office of profit, honor or trust, under this Government.

Sec. 5. The Electors, and members of the the General Council shall, in all cases except those of treason, felony, or breach of the peace, be privileged from arrest during their attendance at election, and at the General Council, and in going to, and returning from, the same.

Sec. 6. In all elections by the people, the electors shall vote *viva voce*. Electors for members to the General Council for 1828, shall be held at the places of holding the several courts, and at the other two precincts in each District which are designated by the law under which the members of this Convention were elected; and the District Judges shall superintend the elections within the precincts of their respective Court Houses, and the Marshals & Sheriffs shall superintend within the precincts which may be assigned them by the Circuit Judges of their respective Districts, together with one other person, who shall be appointed by the Circuit Judges for each precinct within their respective Districts; and the Circuit Judges shall also appoint a clerk to each precinct.—The superintendents and clerks shall, on the Wednesday morning succeeding the election, assemble at their respective Court Houses and proceed to examine and ascertain the true state of the polls, and shall issue to each member, duly elected, a certificate; and also make an official return of the state of the polls of election to the principal Chief, and it shall be the du-

[illegible]

I.

1. [illegible]

2. [illegible]

II.

1. [illegible]

2. [illegible]

III

1. [illegible]

2. [illegible]

3. [illegible]

4. [illegible]

5. [illegible]

6. [illegible]

The front page of the first issue of the *Cherokee Phoenix*.

As the year 1828 began, a Cherokee delegation from Arkansas arrived in Washington, D.C. The delegates had been directed to represent the interests of the Western Cherokees. They had been sent on the long journey to Washington to urge United States authorities to fulfill the terms of previous treaties. The delegates came to ask for protection from white settlers who were trespassing on their lands and stealing their cattle and horses. They came to ask for the money that had been promised them for emigrating from the east. They were also there to try to resolve border disputes with the Osage people, who were the original claimants to much of the territory. One of the delegates was Sequoyah.

By the time Sequoyah had settled into a Washington hotel, there were many white people who wanted to see him. News of the syllabary had already spread beyond Cherokee country, and journalists and scholars in Washington wanted to find out something about its inventor.

Sequoyah agreed to interviews, which were conducted through interpreters. One interviewer was Samuel Lorenzo Knapp, a well-known writer of the time. Knapp later gave lectures to audiences about the remarkable man he had met. Parts of Knapp's lecture were reprinted in newspapers, and Sequoyah's fame grew.

Knapp described Sequoyah as a serious and reflective man. He said the inventor paused after each question was asked, sometimes drawing on his long pipe as he thought about his reply. Knapp worked those replies into the story of Sequoyah's "astonishing dis-

A picture dictionary in Cherokee, late nineteenth century.

covery"—the process of trial and error, the long labor, the ridicule of neighbors, the effort to make the value of the invention known, the understanding that reading and writing were necessary if Indians were ever to "advance in knowledge" as white people had done.

Knapp called Sequoyah the American Cadmus. The nickname would be picked up by other writers expressing enthusiasm for Sequoyah's genius. Cadmus was a figure from Greek mythology. It was said that he founded the ancient city of Thebes in central Greece and brought the Phoenician alphabet (the alphabet that is the basis of the Roman one that is used for English) to Greece.

Knapp was sympathetic to the Indian cause. But he could not conceal his surprise that an Indian—especially an Indian who had not taken up the ways of whites—had managed such a remarkable intellectual feat. It amazed Knapp that the so-called American Cadmus was an uneducated Indian, who "adhered to all the customs of his country . . . was dressed in all respects like an Indian," and lived in the same "state of nature" as other Indians.

Another interviewer was Jeremiah Evarts, an influential missionary leader. Evarts, too, was impressed that the man of genius spoke only the Cherokee language. He described Sequoyah as "about fifty years old, modest in appearance . . . and dressed in the costume of his country."

The other Cherokee delegates in Washington were dressed in the American style. Sequoyah's clothing style, as his interviewers

This pencil sketch was copied from the portrait painted by Charles Bird King. The sketch was given to Sequoyah before he left Washington, D.C., and it hung in his cabin for many years. It has been passed down through his wife's family to its present owner. The medal around Sequoyah's neck was given to him by President John Quincy Adams. Such presidential medals were commonly given to American Indian leaders.

noted, was Cherokee. It was captured in the only portrait known to have been made of him while he was alive. The painter was Charles Bird King, an artist famous for his portraits of Indians. King's portrait of Sequoyah has been widely copied and reproduced. It shows Sequoyah from the waist up. He wears a turban, tunic, and robe. Around his neck is a twisted handkerchief and a ribbon for the presidential medal that rests on his chest. He holds a long-stemmed pipe in his mouth. He is pointing to his syllabary. Sequoyah sat for the portrait that winter in Washington.

It is possible that while he was in Washington, Sequoyah received a copy of the *Phoenix*. It was the first issue of the first newspaper in Cherokee—one to be read and reread and cherished. Sequoyah would greet every following issue with gratitude and pleasure.

Sequoyah and his fellow delegates stayed in Washington for several months. The delegates held negotiations with the United States government. The result of those meetings and talks was yet another treaty. Sequoyah and several other delegates signed their names to the treaty in May. The terms of the treaty alarmed the Cherokees back in Arkansas.

The treaty said that the Western Cherokees would give up their Arkansas lands for land even farther west. The western land was in the region then known as Indian Territory. Today it is called Oklahoma.

Give up the land they had settled! This idea dismayed and angered the Western Cherokees. Many had spent ten years or more on that land. They had built their homes and mills there. They had cultivated fields and raised hogs and cattle. They did not welcome the thought of picking up and starting over. Three years earlier they had passed a law threatening the death penalty to anyone involved with the ceding of their lands. Why had Sequoyah and the other signers agreed to such a thing?

The treaty signers had responded to the persuasive tactics of the United States government: threats and promises. By remaining in Arkansas, the federal agents said, the Cherokees would be forever unsafe from whites pushing onto their land. But in Indian Territory, there would be protected lands for them forever and rewards of money and supplies.

Perhaps if Sequoyah had been someone less respected, the Cherokees would have punished him for signing the treaty. It was said that the signers' lives were in danger upon their return. But Sequoyah was an honored leader and teacher. The anger and disruptions died down, and the people looked to their future. "But what is not to be will not be," wrote a man in Cherokee, in a letter from Arkansas to the *Phoenix*. ". . . The land which has become ours is not far off, and is good land."

In 1829 Sequoyah emigrated west, along with thousands of other Cherokees from Arkansas. His new home was about twelve miles northeast of present-day Sallisaw, Oklahoma. He built a cabin, kept a small farm, and raised livestock. Periodically he left

Sally and the children and headed with a load of supplies to Lees Creek, about ten miles away. There he owned a salt spring. The spring furnished salt water, which Sequoyah poured into kettles and heated. When the water evaporated, Sequoyah gathered up the salt that was left. The process took many days. Because salt was used to preserve and flavor meats, it was valuable and could be exchanged for tools and goods.

Sequoyah made his living from the salt spring. But he was also a teacher. He traveled throughout the Western Cherokee settlements to spend time with learners of all ages. Students came to visit him at his home, too. He welcomed all who wanted to learn, patiently explaining his syllabary. He also taught them about Cherokee history—the ancient stories and ways of life. It pleased him to know that the future would include Cherokees who could embrace both the new skills and the old traditions.

Sequoyah and the other Western Cherokees were called the Old Settlers. They were the first Cherokees to establish homes and businesses in Indian Territory. In a few years there would be many thousands more. Unlike Sequoyah, they would not arrive by choice.

The log house that Sequoyah lived in was still occupied more than a century later, when this photo was taken. The house has been preserved and can be seen in Sallisaw, Oklahoma.

# Seven
# Terrible Times

For years troubles had been building for the Cherokees back in their eastern homelands. The remaining eastern lands of the Nation fell largely within the borders of the state of Georgia, and Georgians resented the Cherokee presence. What had made matters worse was the discovery of gold in the southeastern section of Cherokee territory. Gold fever was raging in Georgia by 1829, and thousands of invaders had come to work the gold fields. There were thefts and violence among the gold seekers, and the state created the Georgia Guard to protect the mines. But soon the army of Guardsmen was being used to enforce Georgia's control over the Cherokee Nation.

Georgia had passed laws to limit the rights of the Cherokees. The state had made it illegal for Indians to speak in a white court, for example. That meant that whites could steal Cherokee cattle and destroy Cherokee homes without fear of punishment. Georgia had also made it illegal for Cherokees to dig for gold on their own property.

The first edition of the *Phoenix* made it clear that the purpose of the newspaper was to "state the will of the majority of our people on the present controversy with Georgia. . . ." It was hoped that the world would take notice of Georgia's restrictions of Cherokee rights.

Georgia wanted the Cherokees out of the state. Many United States leaders also wanted the Cherokees and other Indians of the Southeast to move west. The policy was known as Removal. Its most forceful and determined advocate was the current president, the former ally of the Cherokees, Andrew Jackson.

In 1830 an Indian Removal bill was debated in the U.S. Congress. Not everyone agreed with Jackson's view of forced emigration. The bill stirred up powerful emotions. One Northern senator, Theodore Frelinghuysen, spoke strongly against the bill. His speech, given over three days, was reprinted in newspapers. It brought national attention to the Indian cause. Frelinghuysen spoke about past treaties, broken promises, and the rights of Indians. He accused the United States government of uncontrolled greed. Indians, Frelinghuysen argued, had a moral right to their homelands. The United States itself had been created because of the colonists' opposition to tyrants, Frelinghuysen reminded his listeners. Now the United States government was itself practicing tyranny. The speech gave Frelinghuysen recognition and assured his political future. Unfortunately it failed to help the Indians. The Removal Bill passed the Senate by eight votes. It passed in the

House of Representatives by five votes.

In 1832 Georgia held a land lottery for white settlers. Holders of winning tickets were given large tracts of Cherokee land—160 acres of farmland or 40 acres of mining territory. The Cherokee occupants of the land were forced out of their homes, or forced to become rent-paying tenants to the new owners.

The Cherokee Nation had by this time united under the leadership of its dedicated principal chief, John Ross. Ross was to lead the Cherokees for the next thirty-four years, often facing arrest and threats. Now his job was to travel to Washington and elsewhere to gather legal and financial support in the fight against Removal.

The Cherokees became the only Indians of the Southeast who refused to sign a treaty of Removal. In all the other nations—Creek, Choctaw, Chickasaw, Seminole—there were people who had been pressured to sign agreements to leave their land. Only the Cherokee Nation held on, stubborn and insistent.

But Andrew Jackson and his agents were also stubborn. They threatened a bleak future for those who refused to move. They promised rewards to those who would agree to a Removal treaty. Certain wealthy Cherokees began to allow themselves to be persuaded. They began to see that the Cherokees were doomed if they stayed in the East, that Chief John Ross was clinging to an impossible hope. They began to talk about exchanging existing lands for new lands in the West.

John Ross.

One person with a changing viewpoint was Elias Boudinot. He resigned as editor of the *Phoenix*, no longer able to support its statements against Removal. The newspaper continued to be published, though less regularly. Then one day in 1834, the Georgia Guard stormed the office and hauled the press away.

Elias Boudinot's view was shared by another man, a cousin who owned much property. John Ridge had also been educated in the North. He and his father, the influential leader The Ridge, became open to the idea of protecting their interests and negotiating a treaty. These three men formed the core of a small faction favoring Removal. In December of 1835, they signed the Treaty of New Echota with the federal commissioner. They agreed to exchange all Cherokee territory east of the Mississippi for western lands and five million dollars.

The twenty Cherokee signers of the Treaty of New Echota did not speak for the majority of the Cherokees. Chief John Ross had urged everyone to stay away from the meeting. And Ross was clearly the representative of the people. The signing was followed by furious debate in the press and in the United States Congress. But when the votes were cast in the Senate in May, the treaty was ratified by one vote. The Treaty of New Echota was to go into effect in two years.

The people protested that they had never made such a treaty. But the sixteen thousand signatures of Cherokee men, women, and children that Ross presented on a petition were ignored.

The people found it hard to believe that they would be forced from their homelands. John Ross held on to hope and conveyed that hope to the Nation. He continued to travel, to ask for public support, and to try to reverse the damage that had been done. The people went on with their lives as best they could in the face of increasing pressure and abuse from white settlers and Georgia laws. They retreated farther from white settlements, built smaller cabins, and tilled their reduced plots.

Sequoyah and other Old Settlers in the West received word about what was happening to their relatives and former neighbors back in the Eastern homelands. The news was worrisome. Years before, they had sensed that emigration would be part of the future of the Cherokees. They had emigrated out of choice. But forced Removal would be a different matter—a sad and frightening one to think about. The homelands in the East might soon no longer belong to the Cherokees. This, too, was a sad and frightening thought. What could be done? White Americans were simply too great in number, and too powerful. Sequoyah could only hope that the outcome would be a just and peaceful one.

As the spring of 1838 drew near, the Eastern Cherokees appealed to President Van Buren to reconsider Jackson's Removal plans. But Georgia threatened war if the Cherokees were not made to leave. Van Buren decided. In April 1838, he ordered Major General Winfield Scott to march his troops to Cherokee country. The forced Removal began.

There were about seven thousand men at General Scott's command, charged with gathering nearly seventeen thousand unarmed Cherokee men, women, and children. The soldiers built stockades to hold the people in preparation for the journey west. Armed soldiers surrounded people's homes and forced the families within to march immediately to the stockades. Men and women were taken while working the fields or walking on the roads. Children were taken while alone. By the time the entire population had been herded into the stockades, summer had begun. As they waited, crowded together and ill fed, they began to die.

About five thousand people were the first to make the journey west. It was June when they began, first by steamboats and then overland. It was hot, and disease spread. There was so much sickness, so much death, that the leaders of the Nation feared there would be few survivors of this forced Removal. John Ross negotiated with General Scott, asking that the remaining Cherokees take charge of their own Removal in the fall, after the heat of summer was over. The general agreed.

So it was that in the fall thirteen detachments of about a thousand people each assembled under their own Cherokee officers. Each detachment left several days after the one before it. Nearly all the detachments went by land.

When the first detachment arrived in the West in January, Sequoyah listened with horror to the reports of their experiences. The dreadful stories continued, month by month, until March,

The Trail of Tears, as shown in a painting by the Pawnee artist Brummett Echohawk.

when the last of the detachments arrived.

By foot, on horses, in hundreds of wagons holding the belongings they had been allowed to gather, the people had traveled the miles and miles of the overland routes, crossing rivers as they came to them. Every day the death toll grew—from illness, exposure, lack of food, exhaustion. Those who reached the ice-filled Mississippi in midwinter had to camp beside its banks while waiting for a chance to cross. With only blankets to protect them, hundreds died.

The average length of the journey was four months. Thousands of people were buried at stopping points along the route.

The journey was to become known in English as the Trail of Tears. The Eastern Cherokee Nation lost one fourth of its people on the Trail of Tears.

Sequoyah listened to the stories of suffering and saw the worn faces and weakened bodies. He heard about the deaths of his friends. Aching with worry, he awaited the arrival of his son Tee-see, who had served as an interpreter on the journey. With great gladness, he learned that Tee-see had survived.

The arriving Cherokees tried to conquer the memories of loss and suffering and start new lives. But there was deep bitterness against the signers of the Treaty of New Echota. The members of the Treaty Party were blamed for the horrors just experienced. There were other disputes too.

In the early summer of 1839, many thousands of Cherokees from the Nation East and the Nation West gathered together to discuss their common interests. Three Western chiefs were there to welcome the emigrants. Sequoyah was also there, as a representative of the Old Settlers.

The Eastern Cherokees under John Ross wanted to preserve their form of government. The Western Cherokees—the Old Settlers—were suddenly in the minority. But they did not want to be ruled by the newcomers. They had their own ways of doing things. When John Ross made it clear that he intended to set up a new government, the Western chiefs decided to disband the meeting.

Sequoyah felt torn in two. To be Cherokee meant to seek balance in the world, to embrace harmony. He had known that even as a small boy feeling the shared joy at the Green Corn ceremonies. His people must not be divided in this way. The only chance for unity lay in communication. The factions had to keep talking, even if they could not agree easily. Hurriedly he joined with an Eastern Cherokee leader, the Reverend Jesse Bushyhead, to gather all the groups together again and propose another council. It was necessary "for the peace and security of the whole people," Sequoyah said. His arguments persuaded the people, and they agreed to meet again.

On July 1, 1839, two thousand Cherokees assembled about a mile from the Illinois River, to hold a second council at Illinois Camp Ground. John Ross and the other Eastern chiefs were there, but the three Western chiefs had refused to attend. Sequoyah, serving as President of the Western Cherokees, met with John Ross and wrote a hopeful letter, in Cherokee, to the Western chiefs:

*We, the old settlers, are here in council with the late emigrants, and we want you to come up without delay, that we may talk matters over like friends and brothers. These people are here in great multitudes, and they are perfectly friendly towards us. They have said, over and over again, that they will be glad to see you, and we have full confidence that they will receive you with all friendship. There is no drinking here to disturb the peace, though there are upward of two thousand people on the ground. We send you these few lines as friends, and we want you to come on without delay, and bring as many of the old settlers as are with you; and we have no doubt but we can have all things amicably and satisfactorily settled.*

Sequoyah's letter persuaded one of the Western chiefs to come.

At the Illinois Council, they found agreement: A single Cherokee Nation must be made by uniting the Nations East and West. As Sequoyah said in a speech read to the assembly, the forced emigration had resulted in "bringing together again the two branches of the ancient Cherokee family." It was important that the branches unite and create a government "adapted to their present condition and providing equally for the protection of each individual in the enjoyment of his rights."

A written document made the act of union official. Signing the document, as President of the Western Cherokees, was Sequoyah. He marked an X beside his English name, George Guess. Signing as President of the Eastern Cherokees was Ah-gee-lee, using his English name—George Lowrey. Other leaders also signed, and the East-West Nation was created.

Meetings continued, and in September of 1839 the new Cherokee Nation adopted a constitution. Sequoyah was one of its signers.

# Eight
# A Final Journey

Sequoyah was an old man when he stood at the 1839 councils and spoke of peace and unity. He was a wise elder, someone to be given admiration, attention, respect. He had achieved great things for his Nation. But he had dreams of accomplishing more.

Among the ancient stories passed down from generation to generation was one that told of a lost band of Cherokees. These people had been separated from the body of Cherokees centuries before and had settled, it was said, somewhere in Mexico. Perhaps Sequoyah was now thinking about the descendants of those ancient Cherokees. Or perhaps he was thinking of more recent emigrants. A large band of Cherokees who had lived in Texas had just been forced out by the Texans. Some of the people had rejoined the Nation in Indian Territory, but others had moved to Mexico.

Sequoyah knew that there were Cherokees in Mexico. He set himself the task of finding them. He would teach them to use the syllabary. He would bring them the gift of literacy. Reading and writing in the Cherokee language would unite all his people, wherever they lived.

In the summer of 1842, when Sequoyah was more than seventy years old, he began his secret preparations for the long journey. He gathered eight companions, all younger men. Among them was his son, Tee-see Guess, and a trusted friend known as The Worm. They loaded up three packhorses with supplies and headed south on horseback.

After days of travel Sequoyah began to feel ill. He had trouble swallowing and could not eat any of the venison his companions offered him. Pains had begun in his chest and were spreading to other parts of his body. He managed to travel to a village, where the head man, Oo-till-ka, was known for his generosity. Oo-till-ka welcomed Sequoyah, gave him a lodge, and made sure that nourishing food was prepared for him.

Sequoyah rested and then called his companions to his side. "My friends, we are a long way from our homes," he told them. "I am very sick and may long remain so before I recover. Tomorrow, therefore, I wish you all to return home, except my son and Worm." The six young men agreed to Sequoyah's proposal. The Worm, Tee-see, and Sequoyah would journey on together when Sequoyah's health improved.

When Sequoyah felt stronger, the urge to push on grew stronger, too. He thanked his generous host and gave him presents of tobacco and other small items. Then the small party set out again for Mexico.

They traveled for many days. They camped by running water, hunted for game, and found bee trees to keep up their supply of honey. One night their horses were stolen.

Sequoyah knew he could not continue long by foot. The goal of Mexico—although weeks away—was within reach. Sequoyah's desire to reach that goal was powerful. "If I die, you can do what seems best," Sequoyah told The Worm. "But while I am alive, be guided by me."

Sequoyah asked his companions to find him a safe hiding place and leave him with a supply of food. He told them to travel on to the nearest Mexican settlement to find other horses.

Sequoyah's resting place was in a cave above flowing water. The Worm placed a log nearby so that Sequoyah could climb to a higher point if the water should rise to the cave. Tee-see and The Worm gave him a supply of honey and venison that could last many days. Then the two younger men set out for the settlements of Mexico.

Sequoyah stayed in the cave, writing in the journal that he always carried with him and resting when he felt tired. He often felt tired. He often felt pain. He had developed a cough. As the days passed, he began to worry about his son and The Worm. Perhaps they had met with an accident. Perhaps they had been killed. In his loneliness, Sequoyah's thoughts troubled him.

On his twelfth night alone, a rainstorm began. It was severe, and the cave began to fill with water. Sequoyah gathered his blankets around him. He filled his pockets with as many items as he could. Then he climbed the log to a higher ledge. Perching there, he felt the water rising rapidly around him. The cave was no longer safe. He climbed from the ledge outside into the storm. He spent the night huddling under a tree while the sky poured water on him.

In the morning Sequoyah found a dry place to make a fire. He warmed himself and dried his clothes. It was two days before the water in the cave subsided enough for him to see that all his belongings had been washed away. He followed the stream and found his saddle bags wrapped around a small tree. Inside were his precious papers and a few other items. Then he saw his tent and three blankets. Farther downstream he found one of his brass kettles. All else was gone. But Sequoyah's main feeling was relief. Ill health like his, he realized, would have confined most people to their beds. But he had somehow found the strength to save his life.

For food he shaved off bits of meat from the deerskins that his companions had left him. He had no gun with which to hunt for a new supply of meat. He felled a couple of bee trees laboriously with a small tomahawk and gathered the honey. He wrote a note describing what had happened and tied it to a log leaning against a tree. Then he began walking toward Mexico. Perhaps, if his companions were still alive, they would find him. He would leave a smoke trail for them by burning grass.

It was while taking a break from building a raft for a river crossing that Sequoyah came upon a party of three men who said they were Delawares. "I am a Cherokee," Sequoyah replied. The men befriended him. They wanted to take him to his home, but Sequoyah tried to talk them into going with him to Mexico. They could not agree to travel so far out of their way, but they gave

Modern Cherokee artist Bob Annesley's interpretation of Sequoyah pondering his syllabary. The smoke from his pipe forms the characters of his signature.

Sequoyah meat and a horse.

As Sequoyah continued his journey on horseback, Tee-see and The Worm were on their way back to the cave. They had traveled to San Cranto in Mexico, where they had found a fellow Cherokee, The Standing Rock. The Standing Rock had told them of a Cherokee village about ten miles away, which they had visited. Seven of the villagers were now traveling back with them to find Sequoyah. They were within a few miles of Sequoyah's cave when they came upon the footprints of a man going in the opposite direction. Tee-see and The Worm were immediately worried, because the tracks had been made by a man who walked with a limp and used a stick for support. Why had Sequoyah left the safety of the cave? They hurried to the cave and found the answer in the characters of Sequoyah's syllabary, in the message he had left for them.

The men tracked the footprints. Suddenly there were hoofprints. Was Sequoyah on horseback now?

At last several of the party came upon an old man sitting alone quietly by a fire. It was Sequoyah. When he learned that his companions were on their way, his eyes brightened. The journey could continue.

The group camped for a while and then set out once again for the Mexican village of the Cherokees. When they were finally welcomed there, Sequoyah was joyful. But he was also ill. Too weak to move around, he had to lie down indoors. His health worsened. He coughed constantly. He had sent his companions on a mission to recover their horses back among the Wichitas, and he waited for their return. The weeks passed, and they were delayed. They were never to see him alive again.

One day in August his hosts were preparing a meal he had asked for, and when they came to deliver it, he was dead. Sequoyah was buried in a Mexican town called San Fernando, about a year after his departure from Indian Territory.

Back in the Nation, no one knew what had happened to Sequoyah. Three years after his disappearance, the National Council sponsored a search. They hoped the honored man might still be alive.

One of the searchers, Oo-no-leh, soon wrote a letter in Cherokee to the Council. He said that he had gone as far as Red River when he had come upon several Cherokees returning from Mexico, including The Worm and The Standing Rock. The Standing Rock had been with Sequoyah in his final sickness and had witnessed his death and burial. "It will be useless for me to proceed further," wrote Oo-no-leh. "I will return home. He is dead without a doubt."

In September of 1844, the first issue of a new Cherokee newspaper, the *Cherokee Advocate*, appeared. This weekly, with articles in both English and Cherokee, would be published through 1853, and from 1870 to 1906. One issue would eventually give The Worm's account of Sequoyah's final quest.

The *Cherokee Advocate* was printed on a new press that had been brought to the Nation West in 1835. Over the years the press would produce many publications and millions of pages of text in Sequoyah's syllabary.

Sequoyah's fame spread beyond the Cherokee Nation, to the rest of the United States and to Europe. His name was known by people who would never use the syllabary, who would never even hear the Cherokee language spoken. His accomplishment—the singlehanded invention of a writing system—was something for all to marvel at. But there was more than the syllabary to capture the attention of the world outside the Nation. Sequoyah had unusual combinations of qualities—of curiosity and patience, of talent and diligence, of imagination and wisdom. He held on to hope during times of despair. He gave his people tools for the future while teaching them to treasure the past.

This painting of Sequoyah, by Charles Banks Wilson, hangs in the Oklahoma State Capitol.

The sculptor who began this project was Vinnie Ream, one of the most famous sculptors in the U.S. capital. Vinnie Ream died in 1916, before she could complete her work of Sequoyah, so it was largely done by the sculptor George J. Zolnay. To capture the grandeur he felt his subject deserved, he took an artist's liberties. As a result, this is not a true likeness and does not show Sequoyah as he looked and dressed.

# And Then . . .

Four years after Sequoyah's disappearance, an Austrian botanist gave scientific names to two soaring trees native to California. The botanist wanted to name the trees in honor of an Indian, so he chose a Cherokee man of widespread fame—Sequoyah. The trees are the *Sequoia gigantea* ("giant sequoia") and *Sequoia sempervirens* ("ever-green sequoia," or the redwood), both commonly called sequoias.

In 1905 representatives of the American Indian nations met together to draft a constitution for a separate Indian state. Their meeting was called the Sequoyah Constitutional Convention, and the name of their proposed state was Sequoyah. The proposal for a separate state was not accepted by the powers in Washington, D.C., however. The constitution developed at the Sequoyah Convention was instead soon used as the model for the constitution of the new state of Oklahoma. The area in eastern Oklahoma that had been called the Sequoyah District, because Sequoyah himself had lived there, became what it is still called today: Sequoyah County, Oklahoma.

In 1917, when the state of Oklahoma was ten years old, it presented to the United States a statue of the person it had chosen to honor as its most outstanding citizen. The statue is of Sequoyah.

A U.S. postage stamp was created in 1980 to honor Sequoyah.

# Afterword
## by Duane H. King

In 1821 Sequoyah introduced the power of the written word to the Cherokee people and changed their lives in a dramatic and irrevocable way. His vision and boldness continue to inspire those who dream of a better future.

Sequoyah has been honored in many ways for his contribution to Cherokee advancement. His name has been given to giant redwoods in California, a county in Oklahoma, a nuclear power plant in Tennessee, a presidential yacht, and numerous businesses and corporations. Yet Sequoyah himself remains somewhat a mystery to the general public. His life is shrouded in legend and misconception, and it is only through books such as this one that we are able to obtain a glimpse of his experiences.

Sequoyah's achievements are perhaps most appreciated by the more than 232,000 people of Cherokee descent, more than 13,000 of whom speak Cherokee as a first language. Today, the

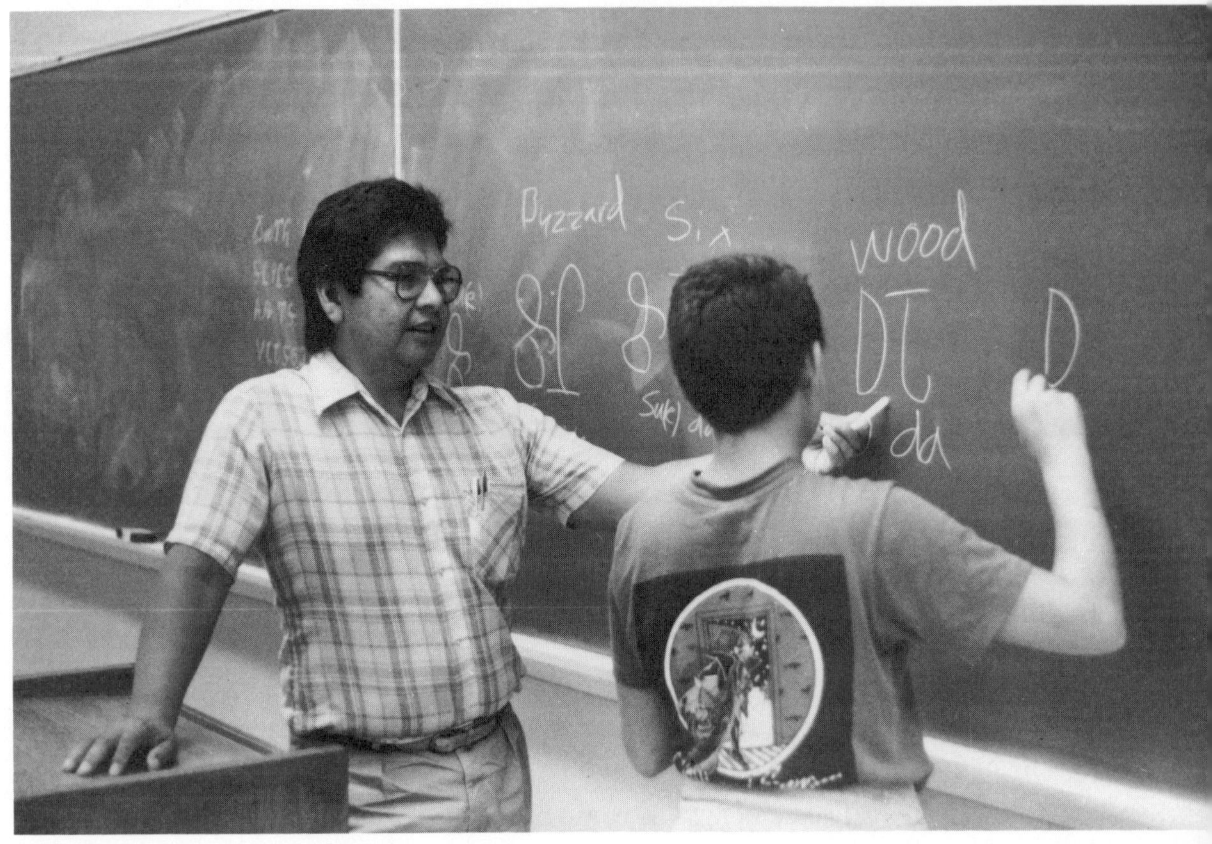


Cherokee language scholar and teacher Durbin Feeling passes on his knowledge to a Cherokee student of today

Cherokee language is taught in schools in the Cherokee areas of Oklahoma and North Carolina. It is maintained in written form in churches, in specialized education programs, and in personal records and correspondence.

Although publications in the Cherokee language today range from legal documents to comic books, the first type was cast to print newspapers and religious documents. The introduction of the syllabary gave rise to the Cherokee *Phoenix*, the first newspaper to publish news in an American Indian language. Subsequently, the printing of Cherokee laws promoted the advancement of tribal government, while Christianity was spread through the translation of the Bible and hymnals. Between 1835 and 1861, more than 13,890,000 pages of books, tracts, pamphlets, and passages from the Bible were printed in Cherokee.

Today this wealth of information in the Cherokee language exists as the result of a goal Sequoyah envisioned almost two hundred years ago. Sequoyah dreamed that his people would prosper through education even though he himself had no formal schooling. His objective was simple. He wanted to create a writing system for the Cherokees. He understood the concept of literacy and had seen others convey thought by marking on paper. This skill, he believed, would unlock the knowledge of the world.

Sequoyah is the only individual in five thousand years of recorded history known to have devised a complete writing system without first being literate in some language. The feat is even more remarkable considering that the language with which he was working is one of the most structurally complex languages in North America. In the Cherokee language, multiple units of meaning are linked together to form words. Every regular Cherokee verb has over twenty-one thousand possible forms.

Within a few months of the introduction of the syllabary, virtually the entire Cherokee Nation became literate. Many claimed to have mastered it in only a few days of study. Among Sequoyah's students, the philosophy was "each one teach one." The payment for the gift of knowledge was to share it with someone who had not yet received it. Sequoyah's legacy is maintained today by those who continue to dream, achieve, and most importantly, use their achievements to benefit others.

# Places to Visit

## SEQUOYAH BIRTHPLACE MUSEUM
### Fort Loudon Island
### Vonore, Tennessee 37885

This lakeside museum opened in 1986 and was dedicated at a joint council meeting of the Eastern Band and the Cherokee Nation of Oklahoma. Its exhibits tell Sequoyah's story and the story of the people of the Little Tennessee Valley.

## SEQUOYAH HOME SITE
### Route 1
### Sallisaw, Oklahoma 74955

At this state park, visitors can see Sequoyah's log cabin, his last home, built in 1829. It has been enshrined within a larger brick building. Nearby, a life-sized bronze statue of Sequoyah depicts him as if looking to the heavens for inspiration as he writes the syllabary. The site also includes exhibits of Cherokee history.

## MUSEUM OF THE CHEROKEE INDIAN
## U.S. 441
## Cherokee, North Carolina 28719

Owned by the Eastern Band of Cherokee Indians, this museum has collections of Cherokee artifacts, information about Cherokee history, and audiovisual exhibits.

## CHEROKEE NATIONAL MUSEUM
## TSA-LA-GI CHEROKEE HERITAGE CENTER
## Willis Road
## Tahlequah, Oklahoma 74465

The museum is built on the site of the 1851 Cherokee Female Seminary and features artifacts, paintings, and reconstructions of the Cherokee past.

# Selected Sources

*American State Papers of the Congress of the United States*, Vol 2, 650-654. Washington, D.C.: Gales and Seaton, 1834.

Bartram, William. *Travels of William Bartram*. Edited by Mark Van Doren. New York: Dover Publications, Inc., 1955. (A republication of the 1928 edition by Macy-Masius Publishers.)

Boudinot, Elias. *Cherokee Editor: The Writings of Elias Boudinot*. Edited, with an introduction by Theda Perdue. Knoxville, Tennessee: The University of Tennessee Press, 1983.

Burnett, John G. "The Cherokee Removal Through the Eyes of a Private Soldier." Reprinted in *Journal of Cherokee Studies* (Summer 1978), 180–185.

Carter, Samuel, III. *Cherokee Sunset: A Nation Betrayed: A Narrative of Travail and Triumph, Persecution and Exile*. Garden City, New York: Doubleday & Company, Inc., 1976.

Davis, John B. "The Life and Work of Sequoyah." *Chronicles of Oklahoma*, VIII (June 1930), 148–180.

Evans, J. P. "Sketches of Cherokee Characteristics." Reprint of 1835 manuscript in *Journal of Cherokee Studies* (Winter 1979), 10–20.

Foreman, Grant. *Sequoyah*. Norman, Oklahoma: University of Oklahoma Press, 1938, 1959.

Greene, David. Letter to Jeremiah Evarts, February 11, 1828. American Board of Commissioners 18.3.1 V 5 Item 324. Houghton Library, Harvard University.

Holmes, Ruth Bradley, and Betty Sharp Smith. *Beginning Cherokee*, 2nd edition. Norman, Oklahoma: University of Oklahoma Press, 1976, 1977.

Hosen, Frederick E. *Rifle, Blanket and Kettle: Selected Indian Treaties and Laws*. Jefferson, North Carolina: McFarland & Co., 1985.

Jahoda, Gloria. *The Trail of Tears: The Story of the American Indian Removals 1813–1855*. New York: Holt, Rinehart and Winston, 1975.

Kilpatrick, Jack Frederick. *Sequoyah of Earth & Intellect*. Austin, Texas: The Encino Press, 1965.

——— and Anna Gritts Kilpatrick. "Letters from an Arkansas Cherokee Chief (1828–29)." *Great Plains Journal* (Lawton, Oklahoma, 1965), 26–34.

———, editors. *New Echota Letters: Contributions of Samuel A. Worcester to the Cherokee Phoenix*. Dallas, Texas: Southern Methodist University Press, 1968.

King, Duane H., compiler. *Cherokee Heritage: Official Guidebook to the Museum of the Cherokee Indian*. Cherokee, North Carolina: Museum of the Cherokee Indian, 1982.

Knapp, Samuel Lorenzo. "Invention of Indian Letters" from Knapp's Lectures on American literature, reprinted in *Niles' Weekly Register*. Baltimore, September 5, 1829.

Littlefield, Daniel F., Jr., and James W. Parins. *American Indian and Alaska Native Newspapers and Periodicals, 1826–1924*. Westport, Connecticut, and London, England: Greenwood Press, 1984.

Lowery [sic], George. "Notable Persons in Cherokee History: Sequoyah or George Gist." Introduction and transcription by John Howard Payne (1835). *Journal of Cherokee Studies* (Fall 1977), 385–393.

McKenney, Thomas L., and James Hall. "Sequoyah, the Inventor of the Cherokee Alphabet." *Biographical Sketches and Anecdotes of Ninety-five of 120 Principal Chiefs from the Indian Tribes of North America*. U.S. Department of the Interior, Bureau of Indian Affairs, 1838.

Monteith, Carmeleta L. "Literacy Among the Cherokee in the Early Nineteenth Century." *Journal of Cherokee Studies* (Fall 1984), 56–73.

Mooney, James. *Myths of the Cherokee*. Washington, D.C.: Bureau of American Ethnology, Nineteenth Annual Report, 1897–1898.

Nyerges, Christopher. "Modern-Day Sequoyah: Durbin Feeling." *Native Peoples: The Arts and Lifeways* (Fall 1989), 48–52.

Perdue, Theda. *The Cherokee*. Indians of North America series. Frank W. Porter III, General Editor. New York: Chelsea House Publishers, 1989.

Randolph, J. Ralph. *British Travelers Among the Southern Indians, 1660–1763*. Norman, Oklahoma: University of Oklahoma Press, 1973.

"Southern Indians East of the Mississippi." Section III of *Transactions and Collections of the American Antiquarian Society* Vol II. Cambridge, Massachusetts: American Antiquarian Society, 1836.

Starkey, Marion L. *The Cherokee Nation*. New York: Russell & Russell Publishers, 1946, 1972.

Starr, Emmet. *Starr's History of the Cherokee Indians.* Edited by Jack Gregory and Rennard Strickland. (Reprint of 1922 edition.) Fayetteville, Arkansas: Indian Heritage Association, 1967.

Sturtevant, William C., editor. "John Ridge on Cherokee Civilization in 1826." *Journal of Cherokee Studies* (Fall 1981), 79–91.

Vanderwerth, W. C. *Indian Oratory: Famous Speeches by Noted Indian Chieftains.* Volume 110 in The Civilization of the American Indian series. Norman, Oklahoma: University of Oklahoma Press, 1971.

Van Every, Dale. *Disinherited: The Lost Birthright of the American Indian.* New York: William Morrow & Company, 1966.

Wetmore, Ruth Y. "The Green Corn Ceremony of the Eastern Cherokees." *Journal of Cherokee Studies* (Spring 1983), 46–56.

Woodward, Grace Steele. *The Cherokees.* Norman, Oklahoma: University of Oklahoma Press, 1963.

# Index

Numbers in *italics* refer to illustrations.

# About the Author

JANET KLAUSNER has had a lifelong fascination with words and language. Her first book for children was TALK ABOUT ENGLISH: *How Words Travel and Change*, which was named a Notable Children's Trade Book in the Field of Social Studies (NCSS/CBC). She has been a special-education teacher and an editor in the school division of a major publisher. She is currently working as a free-lance writer and editor near Boston, Massachusetts.

DUANE H. KING is currently Assistant Director of the Smithsonian Institution's National Museum of the American Indian in New York City. He has also served as Executive Director of the Cherokee National Historical Society in Tahlequah, Oklahoma, and as Director of the Museum of the Cherokee Indian in Cherokee, North Carolina. Dr. King has been a teacher of college courses in American Indian Studies and is the founding editor of the *Journal of Cherokee Studies*. He is also the author of numerous scholarly publications on Cherokee culture, history, and language.